Transformed Through His Thoughts

Guy E. Earle

*"Achieve change by replacing
destructive thoughts
with God's Thoughts"*

Christophe's Publishing Company
providing resources to transform lives

Transformed Through His Thoughts
Achieve change by replacing destructive thoughts with God's thoughts

Book Category: Counseling/Christian living/Inspirational/Practical life

Cover design and book layout: Sydnie Montgomery

For Speaking engagements or coaching contact Guy at www.TheGeegroup.com

Table of Contents

Dedication

It is with great gratitude that I dedicate this book to my greatest asset, my lovely wife Charlotte who has always been a solid support and encouragement. You are a Proverbs 31 woman. And to my dear son, you are a brilliant masterpiece of God and I am so proud of you. My prayer is that you will come to a full understanding of just how powerful your thoughts are.

Acknowledgments

A special thank you to the vast number of men and women who have assisted me in life on some level. I am fully aware that man is not an island and God has blessed me to have been enriched by some outstanding individuals.

To my Mother, thank you for your awesome example of how to transform your life and for your constant support and priceless counsel. To Dad, you have modeled what can happen when you fix your mind on your goal and, as a teenager, you provided me with the love of a father that very few experience. To my sister, perhaps the strongest of the family unit, thank you for your resilient spirit...I love you.

Thank you to those who have greatly encouraged me or poured into my life. George Ryan, Al Cohee, Jack Allen, Frank Minirth, Robert McGee, Dan Collins, Conway Edwards, Robert Crummie, Lucy Mayberry, Howard Hendrick, Darrel Howard, Charlie Ware, Tony Evans, Elliot Greene, LaFayette Holland, Sonny Acho, Martin Hawkins, David and Anita Simms, Greg Whiting, June Hunt, Elizabeth Gaston, and Karen Smith whose excellence and insight has been priceless in editing Transformed Through His Thoughts. I would also like to acknowledge True Faust who is no longer with us, but present in glory.

Foreword
by Dr. Tony Evans

Guy has brilliantly incorporated a wonderful system through God's word to foster a transformed life. The principal is immersing yourself into God's Word to create change. *"How shall a person keep his way clean by taking heed to the word of God?"* Psalm 119:9

Guy has developed a practical and user-friendly method to assist you in changing negative habits and patterns in your life. By incorporating the principals laid out in this book you are developing a new mind, a mind that is focused on God's word. As you change your mindset, your life will be transformed (Rom 12:1-2).

I am confident that the affirmations Guy has compiled are relevant, practical and can reverse your situation if applied. You can begin to experience a life of joy, abundance and victory by learning how to take captive those thoughts that produce sadness, lack and defeat.

Part I:
How to Use Transformed Through His Thought

Consider, for a moment, the mind. Untrained, it could be compared to a lion on the loose. A powerful, out-of-control creation, which, if not harnessed, can reap destruction. The mind could also be compared with the greatest form of transportation. No matter how sophisticated the transport, without guidance and direction, it will never reach its destination. Still others would say the mind is like a garden, beautiful and full of life, but left unattended, weeds will take over and eventually transform to ruin what was once beautiful.

You hold in your hand now a resource to help you cultivate and keep the garden of your mind. For many people, weeds of hurt, pain, frustration, disappointment, and multiple forms of abuse have sprung up, unbounded, in the garden of their thoughts, that seat of conscious and unconscious thought – the mind. The first step in rooting out those unwelcome visitors is to take control of your mind by becoming aware of and tuned-in to your mind's inner chatter, called thought.

Take a moment to reflect and ask God to reveal your inner thoughts that hinder you from experiencing an abundant life. Are they thoughts of anger, fear, retaliation, jealousy, envy, hatred, sadness, insecurity, etc.? Once you have been enlightened to a debilitating thought, plug it into the pre-affirmation evaluation on the next page.

My prayer is that you will make a commitment to God and yourself to take captive every thought that attempts to persuade you that His ways are irrelevant, and to put on the mind of Christ which will empower you in your daily life.

Daily Monitoring Tool
Pre-Affirmation Evaluation

Prior to incorporating this life changing system, determine in which areas you need improvement by taking the evaluation provided below. Rate yourself based on a scale of 1 to 10, 10 being excellent and 1 being poor. Once you have identified your status, determine where you would like to be, (i.e., "I want to be at an 8 as it relates to having a better grip on my anger.") Then proceed to incorporate the Spiritual Synergy Affirmation system while monitoring yourself daily.

Once you have finished reading Transformed Through His Thoughts, revisit this evaluation to measure your progress. You will be amazed at what you will discover and the new life that awaits you as you commit to daily examine and incorporate this system. If you don't see the change you'd like, I strongly encourage you to re-read Part I which explains the philosophy, purpose and power of *Transformed Through His Thoughts* resource. Once you have a solid foundation of how to utilize this life changing book, you can begin to focus on your specific need and issue as it relates to turning negative character traits we call Saboteurs into godly and positive character traits, which we call Synergies. Spiritual Saboteurs are those thoughts that go contrary to God's thoughts, while Spiritual Synergies are those that agree with God's Word. We can know God's thoughts when we read his Word.

The Seven Spiritual Saboteurs are the result of allowing one's mind to be led astray from what God's Word says. But Spiritual Synergy is experienced when you make God's thoughts your thoughts. Faith is vital to achieving Spiritual Synergy because you must train yourself to believe and trust God's Word, even when it makes no sense and when it goes against your emotions, feelings and thoughts.

Part II provides a user-friendly aspect in that you can read and practice each character trait, or Spiritual Synergy, that you most need to develop in your spiritual journey.

Daily Monitoring Tool

1 2 3 4 5 6 7 8 9 10	Healthy view of self vs. low self-esteem
1 2 3 4 5 6 7 8 9 10	Forgiving vs. unforgiving spirit
1 2 3 4 5 6 7 8 9 10	Love toward others vs. anger toward others
1 2 3 4 5 6 7 8 9 10	Joy in Life vs. depression/sadness in life
1 2 3 4 5 6 7 8 9 10	Courageous vs. fearful personality
1 2 3 4 5 6 7 8 9 10	Patience vs. impatience in life
1 2 3 4 5 6 7 8 9 10	Abundance vs. lack and poverty
1 2 3 4 5 6 7 8 9 10	
1 2 3 4 5 6 7 8 9 10	
1 2 3 4 5 6 7 8 9 10	
1 2 3 4 5 6 7 8 9 10	
1 2 3 4 5 6 7 8 9 10	
1 2 3 4 5 6 7 8 9 10	
1 2 3 4 5 6 7 8 9 10	Overall performance of logging my progress

Please make notes to express how you feel you can improve. Also in the blanks you can list other attributes you desire to improve on and create your own affirmation.

Created by Guy E. Earle

How Your Thoughts Affect You Diagram:

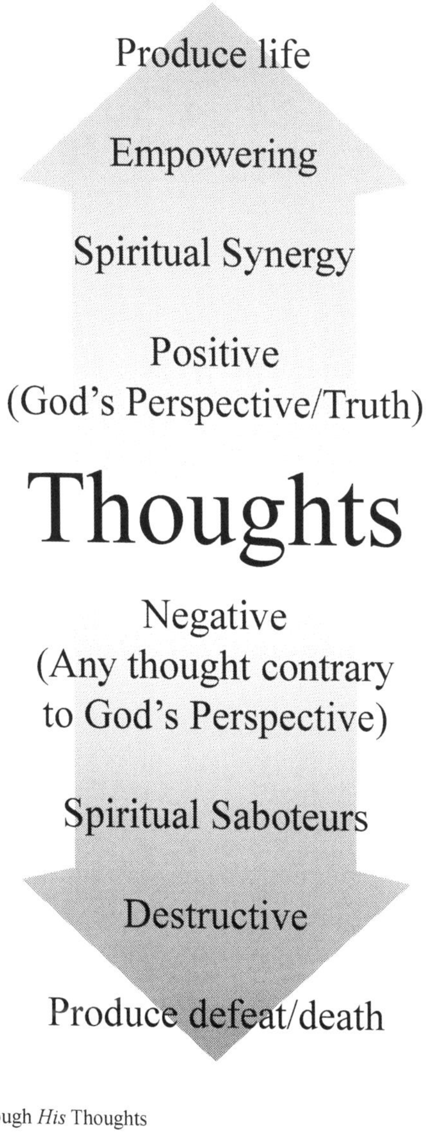

Produce life

Empowering

Spiritual Synergy

Positive
(God's Perspective/Truth)

Thoughts

Negative
(Any thought contrary
to God's Perspective)

Spiritual Saboteurs

Destructive

Produce defeat/death

Chapter 1

Every outstanding feat or accomplishment begins in a person's thoughts, backed up with the white heat of passion and desire, and accompanied with a precise plan of action. It all begins with a seed thought, and a dominating thought holds it together. It is brought to fruition by holding on to the thought come hell or high water.

If we could take a tour throughout history, we would discover a pattern where all significant achievement and contributions began and ended with the power of thought. Jesus Christ, himself, said, "I have come to do the will of my Father." That dominating, overarching thought kept Jesus on the cross. In fact, it was the most impacting thought on mankind because through that persevering thought, eternal life with God was made available.

John F. Kennedy transformed our country with the thought, "Ask not what your country can do for you, but what you can do for your country." Martin Luther King, Jr. transformed our country with the thought, "I have a dream that little black boys and girls and little white boys and girls will one day not be judged by the color of their skin but by the content of their character." The founding fathers of this country transformed our country with the thought, "Our country must be built on a solid foundation." We see evidence of this today penned on all paper currency…In God We Trust! Gandhi transformed a nation with the thought that peace was the passage to harmony and unity.

Mohammed Ali transformed his own life with the thought, "I am the greatest." Tiger Woods transformed his life with the thought of being the greatest golfer. Recognizing the power positive thoughts carry, he told his father, "I need your help with mental toughness. Can you help me by using your Special Forces training because I realize that I can't hit the longest, and I am not better than the other kids, but I can win if I am mentally tough." The wisest man ever to walk the earth, Solomon, coined these words, "As a man thinketh, so he is" (Proverbs 23:7). The essence of this book is that you and I can be transformed through our thoughts. You and I can achieve outstanding feats and accomplishments. Paul taught this in Romans 12:2 when he said, "Be ye transformed by the renewing of your mind."

The mind is a powerful tool and, if left to its own direction it will lead you down the wrong path, particularly if you have been through traumatic events, abuse, injustice and devastating situations. Transformed Through His Thoughts is designed for you to take control of the direction of your thoughts. This book is not intended to duplicate great books like, As a Man Thinketh, Power of Positive Thinking or other books of that kind. Those classic life-impacting books are some of my favorites; however, this resource is more of a practical "how to." The problem with many of us is not that we don't know what to do, but that we don't have the discipline to do what we know.

I want to convince you that your thoughts are like arrows in the hand of a great warrior, they can guide you to the bull's eye of your choosing. This book is a user-friendly method that, when incorporated into your daily life, will teach you to tame your wild thoughts by using affirmations based on God's truth for spiritual reprogramming. The Bible says, "How shall a man keep his way pure? By meditating on the word of God." (Psalm 119:9) In Col 3:16 we find, "Let the word of Christ dwell in you richly." Philippians 4:8 says, "Let your mind dwell on these things which are true, worthy of respect, just, pure, lovely, commendable, excellent and praise worthy."

Now when is the last time your thoughts just went wild, and you had no control over them? Normally our thoughts highlight our present circumstances or past trauma. The Bible says, "…have this mind in you which was also in Christ Jesus." In Hebrews 4:12, God says, "My word is sharper than any double-edged sword, piercing even to the point of dividing soul from spirit, and joints from marrow; it is able to judge the desires and thoughts of the heart." The most consistent barometer for judging and guiding our thoughts is the Word of God.

As a professional counselor, I often see clients whose lives are unwittingly controlled by false beliefs. For instance many may have the thought, "I am ugly and can do no good." That thought is destructive, deceptive, and deadly. You assume this thought to be true, but in actuality it is false. God says that you are made in eloquent wonder by a great God. (Psalms 139) However, if your thought is, "I am smart and sharp," even if that is not your current reality, you will begin to follow your thoughts. You'll carry yourself differently, follow different motivations, and ultimately, other people will see you as you see yourself.

When the children of Israel spied on the Promised Land, they viewed themselves as grasshoppers in comparison to the Canaanites. The Bible says that the Canaanites adapted their view of God's children to the way they viewed themselves. Praise God there were two who saw themselves as bigger, better, and capable of defeating the land giants. I believe their perception changed because they calculated the God factor in their minds. The God factor can be summarized in Ephesians 3:20, "Now unto Him who is able to do exceedingly and abundantly above all I can ask, think, or imagine…"

Satan hates the God factor. He is the father of deception. He desires us to base our beliefs on falsehood. The story of Adam and Eve's failure provides a prime example of the method in which Satan attempts to persuade us to believe a lie. Paul also highlights this fact in 2 Corinthians 11:3, "But I am afraid that just as the serpent deceived Eve by his treachery, your minds may be led astray… ." By convincing Eve that God was holding something back from them and that he, Satan, could provide them with eye-opening knowledge, he planted a seed of doubt. Although the story of Eve is famous throughout history, she is not the only child of God that Satan has picked on. What lie of the devil do you believe? That you are hopeless, helpless, no good, a loser, an addict who will never change? Do not receive his lies. Replace falsehood with the truth of God's Word!

> *"Your destination in life is determined by your choice of thought."* --Guy Earle

> *"Embrace the truth of God about yourself and experience life to the fullest."* --Guy Earle

The opposite of deception is honesty. Satan is the father of lies and deception, but God is the Father of truth and honesty. You can choose to dwell on the lies of Satan or the truths of God. But whatever you choose will be produced in your life.

Satan's lies will hold you captive in bondage, but God's truth will allow you to experience unlimited power and freedom. For, according to John 8:32, "The truth will set you free."

Elephant trainers use chains to teach the infant elephant restraint. As time passes and the elephant matures, his belief that the chain is stronger than he, and can hold him, surpasses the

Transformed Through *His* Thoughts

reality that the elephant could break the chain at any time. The animal cannot break free, not because it doesn't have strength, power, or ability, but because it has been conditioned to believe that it is too weak to break free. Have you been conditioned to think that you are too weak to break free from the chains and bondage that hold you in a state of captivity? Like the elephant you possess enormous strength and power.

Transforming Your Thoughts...

1. **Decide what area of your thoughts you desire to change based on The Seven Spiritual Saboteurs that can hold you in a state of bondage and defeat.**

    These Seven Spiritual Saboteurs affect the wellbeing of a person; therefore, the objective is to reverse these Saboteurs and replace them with Seven Spiritual Synergies:

    a. *Low self-esteem to a healthy view of self*
    b. *Unforgiveness to a forgiving spirit*
    c. *Anger to a loving attitude toward others*
    d. *Depression/sadness to joy and happiness in life*
    e. *Fear/inferiority to courage and confidence*
    f. *Poverty to abundance*
    g. *Impatience to patience and peace*

    From the list above, choose one area where you want to experience change and deliverance in your life, then immediately proceed to Part II of the book, which contains the affirmations that provide the tools to exchange the Seven Spiritual Saboteurs for Seven Spiritual Synergies.

2. **Upon rising, read the chosen spiritual reprogramming affirmation that correlates with your specific need.**

3. **Before you go to bed, Recite the Synery Prayer located in each**

chapter of Part Two.

4. **To create a burning desire and passion for change, write out 20 reasons why you must change.** Please don't take this lightly! This is your motivator; you must create a strong argument and a precept for the reason you want to change. Here is an example: "If I don't begin to view myself as God does, I will continue to let people walk on me and take advantage of me. I have given my personal power away for too long. I am tired of being the victim and am ready to become the victor over my life. If I don't respect myself, how will another person respect me? If I don't learn to value myself, I will continue to attract abusive relationships, and I am determined to not go down that path again."

5. **Pray daily, asking God to specifically assist you with your reprogramming plan and call on His promises.**

6. **Enlist another person as a Spiritual Synergies supporter. Someone who can pray for you and encourage you in your journey.**

7. **On a 3x5 card, write your desired goal in a positive affirming tone and read it at least 3 times throughout the day.**

8. **Prior to falling asleep, plant the affirmation in your soul so that it might germinate in your spirit as you rest.**

9. **Choose relevant scripture that you can commit to memory, examples of which have been provided in each chapter.**

10. **Monitor you progress daily using the provided daily monitoring sheet (extra monitoring can be found in the back of the book.**

Daily Monitoring Sheet

Rate yourself at your current mental state based on a scale of 1 to 10, with 10 being excellent and 1 being poor. As you incorporate the concepts in *Transformed Through His Thought*, using the Spiritual Synergy Affirmation to align your thoughts with God's Word, continue to work on your mind until you are consistently rating yourself between 8 and 10. Please note there will be days that you seem to regress, but don't allow yourself, others, or Satan to discourage you. The road to change is bumpy, and it is almost never a straight path.

Scale	Attribute
1 2 3 4 5 6 7 8 9 10	Healthy view of self vs. Low self-esteem
1 2 3 4 5 6 7 8 9 10	Forgiving spirit vs. Unforgiving spirit
1 2 3 4 5 6 7 8 9 10	Love toward others vs. Anger toward others
1 2 3 4 5 6 7 8 9 10	Joy vs. Depression/sadness
1 2 3 4 5 6 7 8 9 10	Courageous spirit vs. Fearful personality
1 2 3 4 5 6 7 8 9 10	Patience vs. Impatience
1 2 3 4 5 6 7 8 9 10	Abundance vs. Lack and poverty
1 2 3 4 5 6 7 8 9 10	
1 2 3 4 5 6 7 8 9 10	
1 2 3 4 5 6 7 8 9 10	
1 2 3 4 5 6 7 8 9 10	
1 2 3 4 5 6 7 8 9 10	
1 2 3 4 5 6 7 8 9 10	
1 2 3 4 5 6 7 8 9 10	Overall Performance of logging my progress

Please make notes to express how you feel you can improve. Also in the blanks you can list other attributes you desire to improve on and create your own affirmations.

Chapter 2

The Power of the Word

Thoughts are derived from spoken and unspoken words, and words are the foundation of life and communication. Through words, the world and mankind were created.

In Genesis 1, God said, Let there be: (day) light, v. 3; (sky) expanse, v. 6; land, v. 10; vegetation, v. 11; stars, moons, v.14; fish and creatures of the sea, v. 20; birds and all living creatures, v. 24; and, finally, man, v. 26.

The awesome truth is that we are made in the image of God. When God speaks, it happens. Hebrews 4:13 says, "By faith we understand that the worlds were set in order at God's command, so that the visible has its origin in the invisible."

By faith we can speak to those things in ourselves that we do not presently experience or see. It's possible that through our words we are able to produce results. For example, "The worlds were set in order by God's word (commands)." We have authority. He has commanded us to subdue the world like he urged Cain to subdue himself (Gen 4:6). We can subdue bad habits, addictions and those generational patterns by our very words, which help facilitate right action.

Romans 4:16 says that it is by faith that the promise may be certain. God promised Abraham that he would make him the father of many nations. However, Abraham didn't have an heir. How could he be the father of many when he couldn't have a son? But he believed God, the "God who makes the dead alive and summons the things that do not exist as though they already do."

God called into existence the things that were not. This is his creative power, his *ex nihilo* effect, which he demonstrated in creation. The key ingredient to Abram's breakthrough was his faith in God's word and promise. "He was fully convinced that what God promised, he was able to do. So indeed it was credited to Abraham as righteousness." (Romans 4:21-22)

Many of us don't realize or comprehend just how powerful God's word and promises are. *"For the word of God is living and active and sharper than any double-edged sword, piercing even to the point of dividing soul from spirit, and joints from marrow; it is able to judge the desires and thoughts of the heart."* (Hebrews 4:12)

This verse teaches us the concept that God's word is the primary source for penetrating the deep-seated issues of man's heart. The words of God, when incorporated into one's life, are the change agent, the backbone to a successful life. Psalm 1 further highlights God's word as the change agent with the story of the roads chosen by two individuals, one who takes the wicked path and one who take the righteous path. The individual who takes the wicked path follows it to total destruction, whereas the traveler on the path of righteousness enjoys the life of prosperity. The psalmist uses a tree planted by channels of water to illustrate his point. This individual lives in a constant flow of nourishment from the never-ending supply of life-giving water. Just as water produces growth in vegetation, the word of God fosters growth in the individual who applies its advice. Psalm 1:2-3 says, "He finds pleasure in obeying the Lord's commands;

Transformed Through *His* Thoughts

he intently studies his commands day and night. He is like a
tree planted by flowing streams; it yields its fruit at the proper
time, and its leaves never fall off. He succeeds in everything he
attempts."

This concept can be recognized in God's commissioning
of Israel's new leader Joshua in the book of Joshua 1:7-8, who
led God's people into the Promised Land. God gave Joshua a
charge, which potentially was worth billions of dollars in today's
economy. God in a sense gave Joshua a Mega Billion dollar
ticket to experience joy and success. With this blessing God told
Joshua:

> "Make sure you are very strong and brave! Carefully
> obey all the laws my servant Moses charged you to keep.
> Do not swerve from it to the right or left, so you may be
> successful in all you do.   This law scroll must not leave
> your lips (mouth)! You must memorize it day and night
> so you can carefully obey all that is written in it. Then
> you will prosper and be successful."

Again, the power of this book lies in the daily
affirmations you speak to yourself throughout the day because
these affirmations are based on the truths and promises of the
words of God. Remember Psalm 119:9 says, "How shall a
young man keep his way clean? By taking heed to the word of
God." Energy flows where attention goes. As you set your mind
on things above (the things of God), you will gravitate, focus
on, and be prone to conducting life where your mind dwells on a
daily base.

The repeated Spiritual Synergy Affirmations are
designed to help you internalize and reprogram patterns that have
been destructive within your heart and soul. They are a tool to
equip you with the truth of God as you enter spiritual warfare to
change negative habits.

It is quite interesting to me that Paul warns the church
at Ephesus to be on guard because their struggles are not earthly

but spiritual. He goes on to say in Ephesians 6:13, "For this reason, take up the full armor of God so that you may be able to stand your ground."

As Paul instructs the Ephesians on how to stand firm against Satan's schemes, he starts off by commanding them to put the belt of truth around their waists. God's word is truth! However, Satan is the opposite, and his words are false. He is the father of lies and deception. He is very good at it and he has been at it since the beginning of time with Adam and Eve. Do you recall the deception that destroyed man's innocence? Genesis 3:1-5 says, "Now the serpent was more shrewd than any of the wild animals that the Lord God had made. He said to the woman, 'Is it really true that God said, "You must not eat from any tree of the orchard?' The woman said to the serpent, 'We may eat of the fruit from the trees of the orchard, but concerning the fruit of the tree that is in the middle of the orchard God said, 'You must not eat from it, and you must not touch it, or else you will die." The serpent said to the woman, 'Surely you will not die, for God knows that when you eat from it your eyes will open and you will be like divine beings who know good and evil.'"

John 8:32 says, "And you will know the truth, and the truth will set you free." In Matthew 4:1-11, this is clearly illustrated and demonstrated when Jesus, being depleted in physical strength, faces Satan in a spiritual combat.

Satan *distorts* the word, and as the greatest salesman in the world he seeks to sell you a scam. How does he do it? By appealing to your greed, lust, and desires. However, Jesus, having been armed with truth, was able to fight, debate, and defend himself with the word of God. Jesus would rebut with "It is written…" or, in other words, what God really says about the matter is….

As a counselor, I have counseled hundreds of people who view themselves as insignificant, powerless, and unworthy. This may be how they feel, but does how they feel describe or dictate who they are? God says, you are fearfully and wonderfully made. He says you are made in His image, a little lower than the heavenly beings, an overcomer, a conqueror etc. The list of attributes that describe who we are in Christ could continue, but the point is that God affirms our creation.

When we incorporate God's word into our lives it has miraculous power –similar to a cancer patient who has been properly exposed to the proper treatment so she can experience healing. When we properly synergize our thoughts with God's word in our lives, any aliment of the soul can be treated.

For example, take one of my clients who struggled with pornography for over thirty years. I had him memorize Proverbs 5 over an 8-10 week period and to recite and memorize The Mastery over Lust Affirmation:

I am the master of my emotions, impulses, urges and strong desires. God has given me power to subdue the earth and to subdue myself. I am the master of my impulses. No longer will I be dictated by my passions, but I will take personal control over my passions. I will do this by using God's word and God's power to tear down every thought that contradicts his ways. I am the master of my impulses. I praise God because each and every day in every way I am being healed and delivered from my powerless state to a state of great power and victory.

This client is not immune to the spirit of lust but has experienced greater control over the lust verses the lust controlling them. I will express that the client had the greatest success when they immersed themselves with scripture memorization and the mastery over lust affirmation.

When we incorporate God's word into our lives it has miraculous power. For the word of God is alive and what it says it will do. You can be confident that it will be accomplished.

We can trust God, and hold Him to His words and

promises even if we can't conceive, comprehend or understand. If He said it, He will do it.

Always remember: "Now to Him, who by the power working within us is able to do beyond all that we ask or think." (Eph. 3:20)

The Power of Words for Daily Life

The premise of this book is proclaiming, taking ownership of, promises provided in scripture. By hiding God's word in your heart and using His word as a shield, you are in essence warding off the schemes of the devil, as you seek to overcome mental distortions that prevent you from maximizing your life.

Another great example of the power of the word is found in Matthew 8:5-13 which says, "When Jesus entered Capernaum, a military soldier asked for his help. Jesus agreed to go to the soldier's home to heal the servant. But the soldier replied, "all you need to do is say the word and my servant will be healed."

How could this soldier have so much faith in the word? Verse nine depicts his astute comprehension: "…for I too am a man under authority, with soldiers under me. I say to this one, 'Go' and he goes, and to another, 'Come' and he comes, and to my slave 'Do this' and he does it."

Jesus' mouth must have dropped open, as he said, "I have found no one with such great faith in all of Israel." He went on to tell the soldier, **"Go. Just as you believed, it will be done for you. And the servant was healed that hour."**

The soldier understood the authority of the words when they were delivered by one with authority. I Chronicles 29:10-13 describes the awesome authority of God when it says, "O Lord God of our father Israel, You deserve praise forevermore! O Lord, You are great, mighty, majestic, magnificent, glorious, and sovereign over all the sky and earth! You have dominion and exalt Yourself as the ruler of all. You are the Source of wealth and honor; You rule over all. You possess strength and might to magnify and give strength to all. Now, our God, we give thanks to You and praise Your majestic name."

By being made in God's image, we have been given authority to subdue the earth. We too have the power to speak over those things in our lives that do not yet exist. Romans 4:16-17 says, "For this reason it is by faith, that it might be in accordance with grace, in order that the promise may be certain to all the descendents…in the sight of Him whom He believed, even God, who gives life to the dead and calls into being that which does not exist."

It is about time that we stop focusing on what our eyes see or don't see and start recalling, paying attention to and zoning in on the Possession, Power, and Promises God has given us as his children.

Reflection

Have you put your dreams on hold? Has God given you a mission to accomplish, but you, in your mind, can't conceive, comprehend or even see the thing coming to reality? If so, then you are a victim of unbelief. A prisoner of your own mind, which has caused you to be a small thinker with limited vision, and blinded by what you see in the present.

The truth is that you don't have to see a thing to believe it. But, you do have to believe it in order to see it. For it is written, "If thou but cans't believe all things are possible." A prime example is when Abraham did not see the promise, but he believed it. Romans 4:18-19, 21 says "and against all hope Abraham believed in hope with the result that he became the father of many nations." Why? Because "He was fully convinced that what God promised he was also able to do." (Romans 4:18-19, 21.)

You might be saying: "But, God hasn't given me any promises." Well, Satan has done a number on you. God promised in Jeremiah 29:11, "For I know what I have planned for you, says the Lord. I have plans to prosper you, not to harm you. I have plans to give you a future filled with hope."

At the heart of transformation is faith. Faith based on God's word will produce fruit. Faith is not what you see; it is what we know God will and can do regardless of where you are at today. Change is feasible, possible, and available if you believe what God says and have the faith to do what he says.

The Power of Your Words

Proverbs 18:20-21 says, "The tongue has the power of life and death, and those who love it will eat its fruit. From the fruit of his mouth a man's stomach is filled; with the harvest from his lips he is satisfied."

The tongue is one of the most powerful instruments you possess. But, it can produce life or death, depending upon how you use it. This concept reminds me of my military experience in basic training. We were being educated in the use of grenades. Our walk-through was set up to emulate a real war situation. Every one was to get into a foxhole. Now these foxholes were about four-feet-deep and four-feet-wide, and we each had our simulated grenade, which resembled a large firecracker. When they gave us the command to pull the pin, I pulled but failed to hold down the clamp on the grenade. The grenade went off in my hand; I was shocked, stunned, and scared. So, I threw it as fast as I could to avoid any attention. Not to my surprise within 30 seconds the drill sergeant began yelling, "Whose grenade went off?" It took everything I had to admit it was me. He approached my foxhole and laid into me like a Mack truck saying, "Private you just killed your entire platoon!" The moral of the story is that a grenade has the power to save a life or destroy a life. But it all depends on how you use it. Had I used the grenade correctly, it could have protected us and propelled us toward victory. But used inappropriately, as in my story, the explosive power would destroy, defeat, and demoralize. Be aware of the powerful weapon we posses called the tongue. For just like grenades, the tongue can be used to destroy the enemy, but if you don't use it correctly, it will destroy you, and those around you.

Self-Talk

Many people indulge in negative, destructive, and detrimental self-talk. I often see clients who constantly tell themselves that they can't do something, that they are ugly, fat, stupid, or will never get married because no one will ever want them. The onslaught of these destructive words steadily destroys their lives.

Shad Helmstetter has done some outstanding work on self-talk. He believes that the root of our success or failure is in how we have been programmed. "What we have accepted from the outside world, or fed to ourselves, has initiated a natural cause and effect chain reaction sequence which cannot fail to lead us to successful self-management, or to the unsuccessful mismanagement of ourselves, our resources, and our futures. It is our programming that sets up our beliefs, and the chain reaction begins. In logical profession, what we believe determines our attitudes, affects our feelings, directs our behavior, and determines our success or failure." (Helmstetter, p. 20.)

Dr. Helmstetter says that there are 5 levels of self-talk:
Negative Acceptance ("I can't…")
Recognition and Need to Change ("I need to…I should…")
Decision to Change ("I never…I no longer…")
The Better You ("I am…")
Universal Affirmation ("It is…")

Level four, The Better You, is the most effective kind of self-talk. At level four your self-talk is characterized by the words "I am…".

"I am organized and in control of my life."
"I am a winner!"
"I am healthy, energetic, enthusiastic, and I'm going for it!"
(Helmstetter, p. 29.)

What to Say When You Talk to Yourself

One of the most dynamic, inspirational and motivational men I know is Zig Ziglar. For years I have followed in his footsteps of positive self-talk and affirmations. I am not surprised Zig has had so much success in his life, because he has conditioned his mind for success. If he is not quoting his daily affirmations he is listening to an uplifting tape, or meditating on God's word.

Here is a sample of an affirmation written by Zig Ziglar:

"I,_________, am a person with integrity, a great attitude, and specific goals. I have a high energy level, am enthusiastic, and take pride in my appearance and what I do. I have a sense of humor, lots of faith, wisdom and the vision and courage to use my talents effectively.

I am family oriented, open minded, and an excellent communicator. I am a student, a teacher, and a self-starter. I am obedient, loyal, responsible, and dependable. I have a servant's heart, am ambitious and a team player. I am personable, optimistic and organized. I am consistent, considerate, and resourceful.

I am an honorable person who is truly grateful for the opportunity life has given me. These are the qualities of the winner I was born to be, and I fully intend to develop these marvelous qualities with which I have been entrusted by God."

Transformed Through *His* Thoughts

What do you believe you would become if you begin to affirm the marvelous creation you are? One of the most profound principles of the Bible is found in Galatians 6:7, "… for whatever a man sows, this he will reap." Our words are seeds that we plant into our minds daily. The sad reality is that we have been sowing negative seeds of doom and destruction. We must reverse this pattern and begin to sow positive seeds that can result in a productive life.

In my study of the mind and thoughts I came across the work of Masaru Emoto. His work, though controversial, expresses that he has found evidence that human energy, thoughts, words, ideas and music affect the molecular structure of water. This fascinating study is one of the most astounding revelations as it relates to the power of our thoughts and words. In Emoto's experiments, he would write on a bottle of distilled water words like "Thank you," "Love and appreciation," "Fool," "You make me sick," etc. He would freeze the water with these different sayings on them and then examine them under a dark field microscope that has photographic capabilities. The frozen water in the bottles that had wholesome and positive words written on them appeared under the microscope in beautiful crystalline structures. Conversely, the negative and unwholesome words caused crystalline structures that were disorganized, formless, and unappealing.

Emoto believes that when we speak we give off vibrations. If these vibrations, both spoken and unspoken, affect water, what do you think they can do to you? After all, our bodies are made up of a large quantity of water. Scientists say that close to 70-percent of our bodies are made of water.

It is important to know that Masaru Emoto did not use the scientific method when conducting his research (e.g. no use of double-blind studies, no ways to control other variables), yet his work causes one to imagine just how powerful our thoughts and words can be if we take control of them verses them controlling us.

To conclude our thoughts on the power of the spoken word, consider three-time Mr. Olympia Frank Zane in the 1970s who would sing positive, affirming songs to himself because he understood the importance of mental images and words that are spoken and thought about.

A sample of one of Frank Zane's songs is "I know that it's true, it's all up to you. What you see is what you get, you bet, what you see is what you get…" Your perception is made from thoughts, words, and deeds-what you say is what you get, you bet…what you see and say lead to what you do…" (http://frankzane.com/spring_1999.htm.)

Frank Zane's body was sculpted to perfection. He wasn't the biggest, but he was so well defined and proportioned that, even at age 64, he looked like a Michael Angelo statue. Truly as a man thinketh, so is he.

Chapter 3

The Power of Thought

If you want to become the conqueror God created you to be, don't leave your thoughts unattended. Left to wander where they will, your thoughts can lead you down the wrong path, just as a sailboat with no one at the helm is at the mercy of the waves and could end up in dangerous waters.

Our thoughts could also be compared to a computer processor; they both are unseen and difficult to fully comprehend, but they are both powerful forces. The brain is the finest computer processor on the planet. Samuel Wood, Ellen Wood, and Denise Boyd authors of Mastering the World of Psychology states:

"All our thoughts, feelings, and behaviors can ultimately be traced to the activity of neurons in the brain." (Woods, Boyd, p.34.)

Neurons are a specialized cell that conducts impulses through the nervous system. The authors explain that a neuron is activated "every time you move a muscle, experience a sensation, or have a thought or a feeling because an electrical impulse has occurred. The impulses are delivered from the brain to the entire body by the spinal cord." (Woods, Boyd p.39.)

The brain controls the entire body by relating an impulse (command) that is delivered through the spinal cord and the nervous system. Then it is experienced through an outward manifestation (muscle movement, sensation experienced, or a feeling). Like a computer processor it sends data to the central processing unit and then it is manifested when the information is made available.

The brain and its ability to produce thought is a miraculous creation of God that is often taken for granted and not appreciated because it goes unseen by the human eye and is seldom fathomed by the human mind.

Without conscious thought, we command our bodies to move and they obey. For example, we take a step, lift a hand, scratch our back, decide to sit, enjoy a slice of cheesecake and swallow, comb our hair, brush our teeth, or watch the steady movement of traffic on the highway. Every move has been commanded by the control center of the brain, known as thought. It is a refreshing and pinch-me-I'm-dreaming-reality to think that we are powerful beyond measure. God said in Genesis 1:28, "Be fruitful and multiply. Fill the earth and subdue it." In other words, rule, conquer, command, and control. Yet the sad fact is that we are often ruled, rather than being rulers; we experience defeat versus victory; we have become slaves versus masters; and we have allowed ourselves to be controlled versus being in control.

Proverbs 19:8 says, "The one who acquires wisdom loves himself." Literally, it refers to a mind that is willing to work. A mind that is proactive in acquiring truth and acting on that truth experiences productivity in life. If you allow your mind to wander, it can take you to some treacherous and dangerous places. Here's an example of what happens when we lose the reins on our wild mustang of thought…lust turns to porn and porn turns to promiscuity, fornication, and adultery. A wild mustang thought of anger will turn to bitterness. Bitterness will lead to depression, isolation, hatred and eventually destructive words and actions toward others or self. We must learn to master our thoughts so that they don't master us!

As a young man leaving the comforts of my home state, Maryland, I packed everything I owned in a small white Hyundai and headed to Dallas, Texas. Before I left, I knew I was going to Dallas Theological Seminary, but I had no idea how I would pay for it. I also knew that I was going to join Tony Evans' church and that I wanted to work for him at the Urban Alternative. The first thing I did when I arrived in Dallas was to join Oak Cliff Bible Fellowship, Dr. Evans' church, and then apply for an intern position that was open to seminary students. I didn't get the job at first, but in my mind I never lost sight of that thought. Four years later not only was I working at the Urban Alternative, I was working full-time as the staff counselor doing what God has greatly gifted me in.

Another good illustration as to the power of thought is the life of my good friend Kelvin Edwards, who played with the Dallas Cowboys in the 1990's. As a little boy he saw Drew Pearson and the Dallas Cowboys on TV, and he thought, "I am going to be a wide receiver for the Dallas Cowboys." He tells me of how he used to imagine and role-play as a wide receiver in his room on his bed, in the yard, and the playground. He told his family "I am going to play for the Dallas Cowboys" and they would say, "Sure you are…I'll believe it when I see it." Kelvin went on to play college football at a little school called Liberty University, not a typical big league school that would open doors to the NFL, but he ended up playing wide receiver for the Dallas Cowboys.

If you think Kelvin's story has nothing to do with the power of one's thoughts then consider the story of one of my clients who became the homecoming queen of her high school. She recalls, as a ninth grader, walking in the school and seeing a picture of a group of young ladies nominated to be queen. She noticed that there were no pictures of anyone of a different ethnic background. At that moment she pictured herself in the place of those nominated for queen. Four years later when it came time to nominate the queen she couldn't be at school to nominate herself. When she returned to school, inquired whether she had been nominated. The individual overseeing the nominations assured her she had multiple people put her name in. By the end of the process, her picture was exactly in the place she envisioned it when she was in the ninth grade.

Solomon, the wisest man who ever lived, said in Ecclesiastes 10:20, "Even in your thought, do not curse the king, nor in your bedroom curse the rich, for a bird of the air will carry your voice, or some winged creature tell the matter." This verse implies that our thoughts have wings. Therefore, it is vital that we set our thoughts on destinations that are desirable and not detestable. Direct your thoughts toward a worthy goal, and with God, I believe you will be amazed at the place you may end up.

Chapter 4

The Advantage of Spiritual Affirmation

Affirmations are crucial to any form of change or progress.   To affirm is to state positively, to testify, or to declare. According to Merriam Webster, an affirmation is a positive assertion.

Ninety-percent of the time, our self-talk is made up of negative assertions.   These unconscious thoughts rampage through our minds causing a devastating effect.   James Allen in his book As You Think says,

> The mind is a delicate and plastic instrument,
> and responds readily to the thoughts by which it is
> impressed.   Impure thoughts, even if not physically
> indulged, will soon affect the nervous system.   Strong,
> pure, and happy thoughts build up the body in vigor and
> grace. (Allen, p. 54.)

Napoleon Hill in Think and Grow Rich, called this phenomenon of self-talk "Auto Suggestion," the medium for influencing the subconscious mind.

"Autosuggestion is a term which applies to all suggestions and all self-administered stimuli which reach one's mind through the five senses…Through the dominating thoughts which one permits to remain in the conscious mind, (whether these thoughts be negative or positive is immaterial), the principle of autosuggestion voluntarily reaches the subconscious mind and influences it with these thoughts." (Hill, p. 67.)

Affirmations are the vehicle by which an individual may feed his mind nourishment or toxins. The difference lies in whether your mind receives positive or negative affirmations. The reality is whatever you feed your mind will expand, produce, grow and flourish in everyday life. Repeating an affirmation to your subconscious mind steers your mind in the direction that you desire it to carry you. Paul commands us in Philippians 4:8 to think on things which are:

True,
>Worthy of respect,
>>Just,
>>>Pure,
>>>>Lovely,
>>>>>Commendable,
>>>>>>Excellent, or
>>>>>>>Praiseworthy

The reasons our self-talk gravitates naturally to the negative is due largely to our upbringing, lack of unconditional love, poor self-perspective, and other contributing factors. However, we do not have to roll over and accept this mentality of defeat. Rather we can stand up to the bully of negative self-talk and command negative thoughts to leave the mansion of our mind.

In 2 Corinthians 10:3-5, Paul reminds us as believers to tear down every lofty thought that disagrees with and does not

   Transformed Through *His* Thoughts

line up with the truth of Scripture. Proverbs 18:20 says, "From the fruit of a person's mouth his stomach is satisfied." The concept is that one can reap a bountiful harvest from speech that is productive. Truly, our words benefit our lives. Very few of us take these profound words to heart.

Perhaps this verse will enlighten you further: "Death and life are in the power of the tongue" (Proverbs 18:27). Often upon reading such words, we assume that the words that produce life and death are directed towards others. That is an acceptable interpretation; however, consider an even deeper, more personal meaning. The overlooked truth is that our speech has a direct impact and enormous power over our own lives. The very words you speak to yourself can be life-enhancing or life-defeating. The sad reality is that much of our self-talk tends to be life-defeating.

Consider this astounding truth found in Think and Grow Rich!: "the subconscious mind takes any orders given it in a spirit of absolute faith, and acts upon those orders, although the orders often have to be presented over and over again, through repetition, before they are interpreted by the subconscious mind" (Hill, p. 70.)

Here lies the foundation to Transformed Through His Thoughts, the power of affirmations repeated to yourself, until they take root and germinate to produce that which you have sowed, planted, and toiled over in your mind.

There is a nugget of truth that validates the power of repeated affirmations in Exodus 17:8-15. After Moses and Joshua defeated the Amalekites and God told them to create a memorial. They would capture this event by placing it in the Chronicles, better known as a journal, of major events. God instructed Joshua to rehearse what he penned in his journal. According to Exodus 17:14, God tells Moses to capture the victory given by God when he instructs him to, "write this as a memorial in the book, and rehearse it in Joshua's hearing." In other words, God wanted him to go over and over, to repeat and repeat until it became a natural, unconscious part of his person. God also says rehearse these words in a manner that is audible. Wow! There you have it – repeat audibly affirmations that are based on truth to empower you for a productive life.

Another great example of the power of affirmations is found in Deuteronomy 6:4-9. Here, God instructs the Israelites to write His commands and truth on the doorframes of their houses and on their gates. James Freeman and Harold Chadwick in Manners and Customs of the Bible comment that:

"The Jews were commanded to write the divine words on the post of their doors, but they eventually adopted the custom of writing on parchment and putting them in a reed or cylinder that they then fixed to the right-hand doorpost of every room in the house." (Freeman, Chadwick, p.170.)

The direct correlation is that your behavior is a reflection of your thoughts. So if you want better behavior redirect and retrain your thoughts toward the things of God.

The unique ingredient of this book is that the affirmations presented are based on God's truth. God has provided promises in the most well versed life manual that addresses every major issue known to mankind. Promises that when claimed can, and will, produce results far greater than our minds can conceive or imagine (Ephesians 3:20.) These exceeding, great, and precious promises are lavished in splendor in the pages of Scripture.

The success of the Spiritual Synergy Affirmation (SSA) reprogramming system is because we are learning to speak the Word of God to ourselves. Now, remember that the word of God is sharper than a two-edged sword, able to penetrate and produce change like no other mechanism. When we use the word and plant it into our subconscious mind it must work. God said that His word "will not return unto Him void" (Isaiah 55:11).

Psalm 1 says that the one who incorporates the word of God into his or her life will be like a tree planted in water, and it will become extremely productive. The word of God, when planted into the soul of your mind is like magic. It is so powerful that the sciences are not able to explain its life-changing results. It is similar to the power of faith and prayer. In fact, when all three are enlisted into active duty to combat the forces we battle within ourselves, the results are not just phenomenal, they are mind-blowing, out-of-this-world, and truly indescribable. The SSA system has been designed to incorporate the big three: the Word, Faith, and Prayer. In a nutshell, we are claiming God's promises through passionate prayer and backing it up with faith, that God does what He says He'll do.

Rodney Carter, Pastor of Worship at a Oak Cliff Bible Fellowship church, uses a similar technique as the Spiritual Synergy Affirmation system for his personal growth and for creating worship songs. His method is to choose a topic or area that he desires to work on, and then he proceeds to locate a passage of scripture that would appropriately address that particular area.

Once he has determined the passage then he reads and rereads, recites and recites, over and over again. This constant repetition is a form of meditation. The final stage is to begin to put the passage to song. He says by the time he has repeated, meditated, and abided in the word a song appears on his heart. Rodney shares that his marriage relationship had a major storm. He says that during that time he began to meditate on a passage of scripture that could minister to their particular hurt. After meditating on that passage, the Lord gave him a song. Rodney recorded the song, and he and his wife began to listen to it together. He says that God used that song to transform their tsunami-size storm into a peaceful river of love. Truly God's word is able to transform our lives when we replay its life-changing words into our minds.

The Secret Behind Spiritual Synergy Affirmations

- SSA causes you to monitor your life.   On every level those who have any success in life have learned the art of monitoring.   That is a daily routine of keeping inventory of what they possess or desire to possess. Those who are wealthy monitor their money and spending. Those who are healthy and in good shape monitor what they eat and how they exercise. So it is with our thoughts, those who monitor their thoughts will be spiritually, mentally and emotionally healthier.

- It is another way of staying focused on your goal. The SSA is a tool to assist you in managing your thoughts, which are often like the wind. This system, if used as prescribed, will afford you laser-beam-like and purpose-driven focus to keep your outcome, as well as what God has to say about that goal, directly in front of you. When you repeat your spiritual affirmation, you keep the person you are seeking to become at the forefront of your life-changing meditation . . . the miracle power of your mind.

- SSA prevents us from forgetting.   Many of us, if not all, have come across some outstanding principles and truths throughout our lives.   However, we soon forget these truths because we don't have a system in place to recall or to retrieve these life-changing principles.

- SSA is one of the best ways to reprogram yourself through positive self-talk.

- The more direct wording and the more emotion you incorporate in your SSA process, the faster you will realize results, and the more evident will be the phenomenal change mechanism observed by those in your world.

The power of SSA is that you can begin to reprogram the negative self-talk that you have been speaking to yourself for years.   Word by word, you begin to break down the wall of destruction and replace it with a wall of victory, a wall of hope, and possibilities of what your life can become. SSA and positive self-talk are the remedies to the cancerous beliefs, the thoughts that hold you captive, that keep you in bondage, and that eventually destroy your life.

"Every thought we think, every conscious or unconscious thought we say to ourselves, is translated into electrical impulses, which in turn, direct the control centers in our brains to electrically and chemically affect and control every motion, every feeling, every action we take, every moment of every day. Whatever 'thoughts' you have programmed into yourself—or have allowed others to program into you—are affecting, directing, or controlling everything about you." (Hill, p. 53.)

"Change your self-talk through Spiritual Synergy Affirmation, and you will change your thoughts, which, in turn, will change your life."   --Guy Earle

Dr. Daniel G. Amen, is a clinical neuroscientist, child and adolescent psychiatrist, and medical director of the Amen Clinic for Behavioral Medicine in Fairfield, California. In his book Change Your Brain Change your Life, he explains how many problems are related to the physiology of the brain and demonstrates that you can change the physiology of brain through a number of methods.

Dr. Amen shares that our thoughts create the overall makeup of the state of our minds. He states that:

"People who are depressed have one dispiriting thought following another. When they look at the past, they feel regret. When they look at the future, they feel anxiety and pessimism. The lens through which they see themselves, others, and the world has a dim grayness.

They are suffering from automatic negative thoughts. On the other hand, positive thoughts and a positive attitude will help you radiate a sense of well being, making it easier for others to connect with you. Positive thoughts will also help you be more effective in your life." (Amen, p.56)

Now some may think this is a mere exercise in positive motivation; however, it is a known reality that positive thoughts have a direct effect on the mind and body. Dr. Amen preaches that most people don't understand how valuable their thoughts are and, therefore, they leave them to chance. He informs us that every thought we have sends an electrical signal throughout the brain. He says that thoughts have physical properties and that they influence every cell in your body. Therefore, teaching ourselves to control and direct our thoughts in a positive way is one of the most effective ways to feel better. (Amen, 56-57.)

Now that the power of thought has been addressed let's explore how we can change negative, defeating thoughts into more positive and liberating thoughts.

Chapter 5

"Man sees his failure or success, his joy or sorrow, before it swings into visibility from scenes set in his own imagination." *(Florence Scovel Shinn)*

All change begins in the mind, and the mind that produces change is composed of two major components: desire and belief. For example, Proverbs teaches "For it is the mind which houses thoughts, and it is thoughts that determine who you are" (Proverbs 23:7, scripture amplification, mine). Daniel 1:8 says, "Daniel made up his mind that he would not defile himself with the king's choice food or wine." It is apparent that Daniel's discipline and self-control began in his mind.

Additionally, Mohammed Ali said, "Champions aren't made in gyms. Champions are made from something they have deep inside them: a desire, a dream, a vision."

Desire is an innate passion, drive, and focus that comes only from within oneself. Behind every success story is the often-overlooked power of desire to achieve a certain goal. Desire is the soul behind success; it is the fuel, energy, persistence, resourcefulness, and creativity that will be necessary to arrive at your destination. If you remove desire, you will not achieve your directed purpose. As I examine my own life, every success stems from some level of my deep desire.

For example, I wanted to earn my first master's degree in theology, but I was financially destitute with no place to live. That was in 1990. By 1994, I had arrived at my destination! But it wasn't pretty or easy. In fact, there were some very difficult and trying days. I worked my way through seminary on scholarships and part-time jobs. I delivered papers, started a cleaning business, worked construction, and lived like a pauper.

I remember sitting down with my wife and communicating my desire to become a counselor. She concurred, so we agreed I should pursue my second master's degree in marriage and family counseling. We had a family, and our finances weren't solid. But I had four things going for me: a desire, a definite plan, a wife who supported me, and a commitment to reach my goal.

Again, I was working a full-time Job at Oak Cliff Bible Fellowship where I was Director of Missions and Evangelism. In this position, I had an awesome boss in LaFayette Holland (who was hard-nosed and made sure that you were responsible to carry out your mission and duty at work). Still, he encouraged me to finish my second Master degree.

I remember driving across town sometimes three times a day, which was almost an hour each way. I can recall the late nights when I had to counsel at Southwestern Baptist Theological Seminary and get home around 11:00 p.m. But through desire, hard work and the strength of Christ I accomplished my goal. I walked across the stage to receive my degree with great relief, joy and excitement because I had reached the goal I had set out to accomplish.

The Catalyst to Change

Change begins within a person, utilizing the tools and equipment within an individual; it's not something to be found externally. Far too often we give power to the outside forces (other people, opinions, and influences). When we look to an outside source, we give that source power over us.

Therefore, change begins with taking personal responsibility. Shift your focus from others to yourself, no longer blaming, making others your scapegoat, or crediting your failures, lack of growth, or stagnation to an outside force. You embrace ownership by taking personal responsibility.

In the inspiring bestseller, The 7 Habits of Highly Effective People, Steven Covey shared a very powerful concept, "He said in between stimulus and response is space." (Covey, p.69.) My question to you is what is in the space? Let me illustrate. Someone cuts you off on the interstate. What is your initial response? Most of us would have a few choice words, and if we didn't have choice words we might be prone to give a choice finger.

How do you think you would feel after losing control and expressing yourself with choice words and fingers? Probably not too great. If I asked you why did you respond that way you might reply: "Because they made me; you should have seen how they almost caused me to have an accident! I could have been killed!" You just gave yourself a legitimate reason for your action. Unfortunately, we all blame outside forces for our reactions.

Now, lets go back to the question, "What is between stimulus and response?" What is between the outside forces and our personal response? The answer is CHOICE.

When you respond in an unfavorable manner, no one put a gun to your head and said, "Now say some very bad words.' Sure, the outside force was in the wrong, and it was disappointing to you, but your response was entirely your choice! No one made you do it.

When we take personal control over our responses we get "response-ability." This concept is illustrated well in Man's Search for Meaning. In the book, Holocaust survivor Viktor Frankl writes about his experience in a Nazi concentration camp. Everything was taken away from the Jewish prisoners. They were stripped of their clothing, pictures, and personal belongings. The Nazi captors even took away their names and gave them numbers. Frankl was number 119104, but he said there was on thing the Nazis couldn't take away:

"Everything can be taken from man but one thing, the last of human freedoms – to choose one's attitude in any given set of circumstances."

(Frankl, p. 86.)

In Gen 4:3-7, we see this concept of personal power and personal "response-ability" (freewill), in the following story:

Adam and Eve had two sons, Cain and Abel. Part of God's worship requirements was that his people had to offer a tithe, or a tenth, of the profits from their possessions, which He called the first fruits. Cain gave to God from the least of his possessions while Abel gave to God from the best of his possessions. The Bible says that as a result, God was pleased with Abel's first-class offering while he rejected Cain's second-class offering. Like a three-year-old child, Cain threw a temper tantrum. So God came to Cain with some very self-empowering words. "Then the Lord said to Cain, 'Why are you angry, and why is your expression downcast? Is it not true that if you do what is right you will be fine? But if you do not do what is right, sin is crouching at your door. It desires to dominate you, but you must suppress it." (Genesis 4:7.) Wow, God is telling Cain that he is capable of having mastery over this inward battle.

Let's Summarize

The stimulus = God accepting Abel's offering and

rejecting Cain's.

The response = Cain killing his brother Abel (Gen 4:8).

But in between stimulus and response is choice. The choice can be clearly seen when God said, "Sin is crouching at the door. It desires to dominate you, but you must suppress it."

In theology, this concept is called freewill. "God having made man as he purposed means that man has certain capacities (e.g., the capacities to desire and to act)." God felt that, for reasons which were evident to him but which we can only partly understand, it was better to make human beings rather than androids." (Christian Theology, p. 561.)

Once you acknowledge personal responsibility, then you must alter thoughts that keep you from experiencing growth. Remember, the wisest man in the Bible said, "As a man thinketh, so is he." What you think about will expand beyond that initial seed of thought. Whether good or bad, your dominating thoughts will manifest into reality. Paul encouraged us in Philippians 4:8 to think on thoughts that are positive, powerful and praiseworthy. The truth is that many of our struggles and situations stem from self-defeating thoughts. These thoughts often have their roots in childhood. We have been conditioned and programmed to conduct life in a manner that is not favorable to our success. We have bought into lies that have brainwashed us.

Another description of having been programmed and influenced by outside forces and internal dialog can be depicted as a paradigm. A paradigm is a model or a pattern that has been learned. It's important to realize that just because a pattern of thought has been learned doesn't make it right.

As a young child growing up, I was put in the slow-learner's class. My grades were very poor and at that rate it looked like high school would be a real challenge. I began to believe that I was mentally slow. Many of my elementary teachers and family thought I perhaps wasn't cut out for school.

By the time I arrived at high school, I began to do a much better job but still had some trouble subjects. By college I had realized that I wasn't slow and began to do exceptional course work.

Amazingly, by the time I completed my Masters in Theology I rarely received a grade lower than an A, and the same would hold true with my second master's degree in Marriage and Family Counseling as well as my doctorate course work in Clinical Psychology.

I had a belief pattern and dialogue that said I was slow, not smart, and didn't fit with the other kids. However, that pattern was a lie, for I had not learned to adjust to my learning style. In fact I realized I am an astute student who loves to learn. Yet, learning to shift my old pattern was no easy task, in fact I studied and worked very hard to excel. I developed a deep passion for learning and set my mind upon finishing school with a 3.5 grade point average in preparation for my doctoral studies. Then a change began to occur, my grades began to reflect my thoughts. No longer was I focused on what I lacked academically, but I began to focus on the joy and passion of learning and arriving at the destination in which I had planted in my mind.

An old story goes that every Thanksgiving there was a family tradition to cut the tail of the ham off before cooking it. This happened for decades until someone finally asked, "Why do we cut the tail of the ham off?" The reply? "I don't know it has always be done this way." When the family began to research the reason, asking older relatives if they knew the reason behind the tradition, it was discovered that originally the family didn't have a pan big enough to accommodate the whole ham! Just because something has always been done a certain way doesn't mean it's not time to change the pattern.

Perhaps we have patterns, thoughts and models that we adhere to like a family tradition that is not in our best interest. Actually, I am convinced that we do. Therefore, we must research and discover the patterns and paradigms that control our lives, but are not in our best interest.

DISCOVERING Self-DEFEATING DIALOGUE PARADIGMS:

- What external factors have defined you?
- How have others defined you?
- How have you defined yourself?
- Write out your dreams and goals.
- Now list why you think you can accomplish those goals.
- List why you cannot accomplish the goals you have set.

When you understand why you feel and believe you cannot accomplish your goals, you have discovered the defeating dialogue paradigm you adhere to. It is this dialogue that has acted like a dam to you experiencing your dreams.

A client with whom I have worked extensively had a defeating and debilitating internal dialogue, "I am ugly and no one would ever want to be in a relationship with me." These thoughts originated from a number of causes, but a major contributor to the birth of these thoughts came from the verbal abuse of his step-father who told him, "You are fat, ugly, and no woman will ever want you and you will always live with your mother."

When we uncovered the root of these defeating thoughts the new thoughts and emotional remodeling phase was ready to begin.

Once you discover your own defeating dialogue, you must replace it with dynamic dialogue based on God's word, not on how you feel.

Consider the following emotional formula:

- Self-defeating beliefs → defeating thoughts → defeating emotions → **defeated behavior**.

The change factor is in acknowledging and altering self-defeating beliefs:

- A^3 = A to the 3rd power (Attack, Acknowledge, and Alter)

- A^1 = **Attack** self-defeating beliefs
  "I am slow and stupid" **NO!** *You may not be like the other students, but you are special in your own way*

- A^2 = **Acknowledge** self-defeating dialogue
  "I have allowed this belief to rule and control my life."

- A^3 = **Alter** self-defeating dialogue with dynamic dialogue
  No longer will I adhere to the dialogue that I am slow and stupid. But I will alter my dialogue to: "I am sharp, a quick study, and committed to becoming an excellent student."

Dynamic self-talk that is based on God's truth → dynamic thoughts → dynamic emotions → **dynamic behavior.**

Thought Transformation Tool

The purpose of this exercise is to create a log of your self-talk. This means taking a mental note of when and what you say to yourself. Over the next two days you will write down all negative thoughts directed both to yourself and to others.

We will then process this thought in three phases.

<u>Phase I</u>
A. Take a mental note of all negative things you say and think to yourself, perhaps like these:
    1. I don't like myself.
    2. I am ugly.
    3. I can't do anything right.
B. Take a mental note of all negative things you say and think to others (family, friends, co-workers, and strangers):

1. They are stupid.
2. They are fat.
3. They are ugly.

Phase II

Go back and replace the negative dialogue with positive thoughts, for example:

Old Thought	**New Thought**
I am fat and ugly.	I am created in God's image and I accept myself in my present state.
He is stupid.	I will see my co-worker through the eyes of our creator.

Phase III

On a 3x5 card, exercise the self-directed thought transformation. Discovering the root of your defeating dialogue and thoughts can be uncovered by completing steps 1-5 of phase 3. Then in step 6 create a new dialogue that is empowering rather than debilitating. Once you create this dynamic dialogue begin to rehearse it daily and often.

1. Write out your *Defeating Dialogue*	**2.** *What is the foundation of this thought?*	**3.** *Have I always felt this way?*
4. *Has there been a time when I did not feel this way? If so when?*	**5.** *Is this thought working on my behalf? If not, why?*	**6.** *How can I turn the defeating dialogue into a dynamic dialogue that would give me more power?*

Once you have altered the hardware in your computer called the mind you are ready to incorporate the acceleration formula.

The Ultimate Success Formula GPS + E x R²

This formula is new, but the concept has been around and used by Napolean Hill, Jim Rohn, Zig Ziglar, Anthony Robbins and many others. Most importantly its roots can be found in God's word.

GPS + E x R^2
G(Goals) **P**(Plans/Steps) **S**(Super Action) + **E**(Evaluate) x **R^2** (R^1 Replace what isn't working, R^2 Role Model who demonstrates the behavior you want to incorporate)

G=Goals

Where there is no vision, the people are unrestrained.
—Proverbs 29:18

Realize what you really want. It stops you from chasing butterflies and puts you to work digging gold.
—William Moulton Marsolen

Goals set a person on course. Those who have no goals will never know if they have arrived at their destination, for goals are measuring instruments to notify you of the necessary adjustments needed in order to reach your desired outcome. Setting realistic and attainable goals is the foundation to pursing and experiencing change. Habakkuk 2:2 says "Write down the vision! Record it legibly on tablets, so the one who announces it may read it easily."

    Transformed Through *His* Thoughts

<u>P=Plans</u>

Once you have set the goal you must have a plan. Goals within themselves are just statements on a piece of paper unless you strategize how to accomplish the goal. In the book of Nehemiah, after exploring and observing the ruin of Jerusalem, the prophet communicated his vision. "He replied, 'Get going! Let's rebuild.' (Nehemiah 2:18)

It took them 52 days to rebuild the wall. Wow! This was an amazing feat that was accomplished because of God's help and because they had a strategized plan. If you examine Nehemiah chapters 3-6, you will see how each group had a section of the wall to reconstruct. They had a plan and a method to reaching their goal.

<u>S=Super Action</u>

Actions are a vital aspect to reaching any goal. Nehemiah and the builders were able to reach their destination/goal in record time because they accelerated their action. Goals are great, plans are good, but actions allow one to experience the goals set.

"In all hard work there is profit, but merely talking about it only brings poverty." (Proverbs 14:2)

This proverb is saying mere talk produces nothing. Producing anything of value or profit requires effort, toil, work, and action. In the New Testament, Paul told believers residing in Pontus, Galatia, Cappadocia, the province of Asia, and Bithynia "to get your minds ready for action." (1 Peter 1:13a). Paul understood that mere talk alone would not accomplish the work of God. They were going to need to put into action what they knew to do.

<h1 style="text-align:center"><u>E=Evaluate</u></h1>

Action is awesome when it is the right action. However, have you ever acted without seeing fruit or reward? The fact is all action does not produce good results.

Right actions=right results
Wrong actions=wrong results

Often a person will say, "but I have been doing this or that…," but upon examining their efforts and actions they discover that they have been spinning their wheels, an act in futility. Therefore, it is crucial to evaluate and examine actions to determine if it they are profitable and beneficial toward helping them achieve goals.

"But a man must examine himself."
(1 Corinthians 11:28a)

"But each one must examine his own work, and then he will have reason for boasting in regard to himself alone, and not in regard to another." (Galatians 6:4)

"But examine everything carefully!"
(1 Thessalonians 5:21)

There can be no improvement without careful
examination and evaluation.   *--Guy Earle*

All growth stems from evaluation. Evaluation prevents stagnation. Each year, car manufacturers introduce a new and improved vehicle over the previous year. Job evaluations are performed to create growth and productivity. You must constantly measure and evaluate your progress to determine the needed adjustments to produce excellence.

          Transformed Through *His* Thoughts

R¹= Revise Plans and Strategies That Aren't Working.

Once you determine what actions aren't working for you, replace them with actions and plans that are productive.

Jacob, in Genesis 35:2, realized that worshiping foreign gods was not in good practice and was not getting him the proper results for his family.

"So Jacob said to his household and to all who were with him, 'Put away the foreign gods which are among you, and purify yourselves and change your garments.'"

In Eph 4:22-32, Paul clearly illustrates that we need to revise, reverse, and replace old useless patterns with new patterns, behaviors, and actions that are productive.

In 4:22, he says to lay aside the old man and in 4:24 he says put on the new man. This is also illustrated in Ephesians 4:25-32. Additionally, this concept can be depicted by the Michael Jackson song, Man in the Mirror:

> *I'm gonna make a change, for once in my life*
> *Its gonna feel real good, gonna make a difference*
> *Gonna make it right...*
>
> *I'm starting with the man in the mirror*
> *I'm asking him to change his ways*
> *And no message could have been any clearer*
> *If you wanna make the world a better place*
> *Take a look at yourself and make a change*

The final step to change and reaching ones goal is:

R² = Role Models.

Whom you hang out with is a clear indication of who you really are. I was introduced to Dr. Tony Evans in the late 1980s. I began to listen to his tapes and when I went to seminary in Dallas, I joined his church. I knew I wanted to learn from the best. Within four, years I was working for Dr. Evans and traveling with him to Promise Keepers, seminars, and conferences. He has been a key role model for me in ministry.

If you know where you want to go, a positive way to accelerate your arrival date is to find someone who is already where you want to be, then model their efforts and practices. Duplication is not bad, conversely, it is often extremely smart. We don't have to reinvent the wheel, but we can make it our own.

"Not because we do not have the right to this, but in order to offer ourselves as a model for you, so that you would follow our example." (2 Thessalonians 3:9)

"Manoah prayed to the Lord, 'Excuse me Lord. Please allow the man sent from God to visit us again, so he can teach us how we should raise the child who will be born.'" (Judges 13:8)

"Give instruction to a wise person, and he will become wiser still; teach a righteous person and he will add to his learning." (Proverbs 9:9)

In summary, change is a process. Once we root out our defeating thoughts and replace them with dynamic thoughts, we are ready to experience growth. Growth, then, on any level is achieved by setting clear goals, having a clear plan, followed by clear action. Next, you must evaluate the action to determine if it is productive or non-productive. If it is non-productive, replace it with productive, valuable action. Lastly surround yourself with individuals who have produced great results and have experienced success in the areas in which you desire to grow.

Part II: Spiritual Synergy Affirmations

This book consists of two phases. Phase I was focused on revealing how to synergize the Word of God and your own thoughts to change your life. The second phase of the book is a practical tool of how to utilize the Spiritual Synergy Affirmation System to pinpoint areas of your life that need change. This concept is based on incorporating God's Word to combat those thoughts that sabotage your spiritual and emotional well-being. The affirmations provided in chapters 6-12 are designed, rooted firmly in the Word of God, to be used as your weapon of spiritual warfare to destroy every thought that rebels against the truth of God's Word.

I have created and developed these based on my own struggles and the struggles of others with whom I have counseled over the years. Having served as the Staff Counselor for the Urban Alternative radio program with Dr. Tony Evans and the Director of Counseling at Oak Cliff Bible Fellowship, I have seen a pattern in the area where most of us have struggles. The list provided is not exclusive, but it highlights key areas where we as believers have allowed ourselves, the world, and the enemy to defeat us. The key to this second phase is using the affirmations. The affirmations are broken up into the unabridged affirmation and the abridged affirmation. They are provided in the second half of the book at the end of each chapter. Put the abridged affirmation on a 3x5 card to carry with you and use as a quick reminder of the truth you are programming into yourself. Use the Synergy Prayer at the end of each chapter to speak God's Word back to God and show Him that you align your thoughts with His.

The Solution to Destructive Thoughts

When you have a thought that is spiritually destructive you must put it through the "Thought Filtration Process Formula"

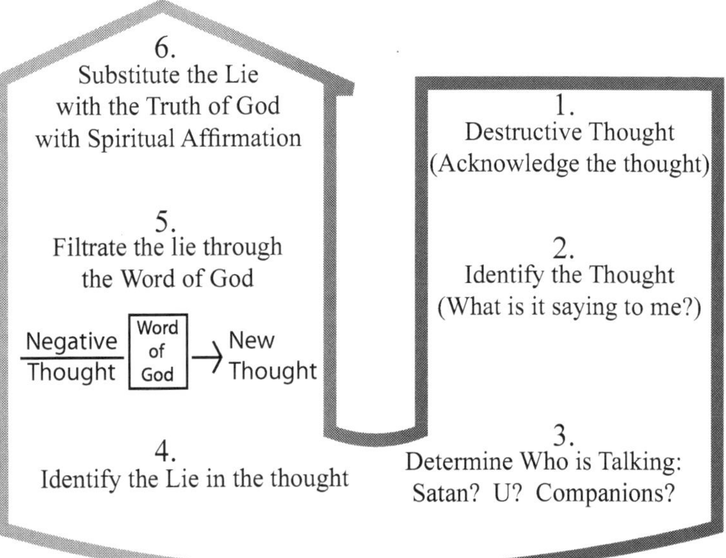

Chapter 6

Low self-esteem is an internal evaluation of how *you* feel and how you interpret your own value and worth. *Notice that the process begins with you.* Your personal perspective is internalized. You automatically assume the rest of the world sees you the same way you see yourself.

Victory over low self-esteem begins with realizing it isn't all about you. But it *is* all about *God*, and how *He* views *you.*

If your view of yourself is not favorable or your perspective of yourself is negative, destructive and overly critical then you must decide to replace the demoralizing thoughts with empowering thoughts. This can be accomplished by bringing to your memory how God views you, what he says about you and how vast his love is for you.

REFLECTIVE QUESTIONS:

- Whom do you believe more?
- What you think about yourself or what God says about you?

"Some trust in chariots, and some in horses: but we will remember the name of the LORD our God." Psalm 20:7

Affirmation

I am loved deeply by God. His thoughts of me are constant, non-stop (Psalm 139:17-18,) and He never takes His eyes off of me (He never sleeps or slumbers). I am so very special to Him; He says that I am precious and all His thoughts are pleasant, pleasing and palatable toward me. His thoughts toward me are so precious that they outnumber the sand on the seashore (Psalm 139:17).

Psalm 86:15 – "You, O Sovereign Master, are a compassionate and merciful God. You are patient and demonstrate great loyal love and faithfulness."

I am fully loved and accepted regardless of my performance, success, or lack of success, achievement or lack of achievement, accomplishments, or lack of accomplishments, failures, flaws, or follies. There is nothing I can do or say to separate me from God's unfailing love . . . neither death, nor life, nor angels, nor heavenly rulers, nor things present, nor things to come, nor powers, nor depth, nor anything else in creation will be able to separate me from the love of God. I am fully

*accepted and I receive, recognize and rejoice in this
awesome truth.*

*I am confident in myself regardless of what
others may say to me or about me. My assurance
and confidence rest in the fact that I am made in the
image of God. I obtain the ability to perform, produce,
and possess. Why? Because God has given me the
command to subdue the earth and with the command He
has provided the means to demand, to take a stand, to
control, to take hold, to captivate, and not to placate.*

Psalm 8:4-6 "Of what importance is mankind, that
you should pay attention to them, and make them almost like
the heavenly beings? You grant mankind honor and majesty.
You allow them to rule over your creation, you have placed
everything under their authority."

*I choose today to focus on the power,
potential and position God has granted to
me. No longer will I live as an insignificant,
powerless person. For I am made of greatness!
I am a royal priesthood made to rule. I am
confident because God believed in me enough
to give me a position of power. Regardless if I
feel I deserve it or not, God in His wisdom has
promoted me to a place of majesty.*

Abridged Affirmation

*I am loved deeply by God. My assurance
and confidence rest in the fact that I am made
in the image of God. I am made of greatness!
Regardless if I feel I deserve it or not, God
in His wisdom has promoted me to a place of
majesty.*

Synergy Prayer:

Dear Lord,
I thank you that I am fearfully and wonderfully made,
I thank you that I am a little lower than the Heavenly
beings, I thank you that your thoughts toward me are
so precious. Now, by faith I accept this truth because
you said it, and because you said it I believe it, even if I
can't conceive it.

Transformed Through *His* Thoughts

Chapter 7

Victory Over Anger

Unlike unforgiveness, which is always negative and damaging, anger serves both good and bad purposes. The Bible says in Ephesians 4:26, "Be angry and sin not." So, obviously, the Lord says a person can be angry without sinning.

If you were wronged, treated unfairly or have experienced injustice, you have a right to be angry.

Anger is appropriate when someone has violated your body, person, possessions, or feelings. The offender has failed to show and give you the proper respect you deserve as a creation of God.

However, just as someone can be angry without sinning, often many are angry and sin. The sin is not in the feeling of hurt or remorse. The sin is when one takes justice and retribution into their own hands.

This act of playing God is the real sin. It is saying, "God, I will take matters into my own hands, I will repay, I will revenge, I will retaliate, I will re-inflict, I will re-injure."

Anger can lead to inappropriate action. This inappropriate action is normally introduced by an inappropriate feeling and emotion. Anger is an emotion, but an emotion gone wild will lead to inappropriate action.

Think back to the story of Cain and Able. In Genesis 4: 6-8 we see:

Then the Lord said to Cain, 'Why are you angry, and why is your expression down cast? Is it not true that if you do what is right, you will be fine? But if you do not do what is right; sin is crouching at the door. It desires to dominate you, but you must suppress it....Cain said to his brother Abel, "Let's go out to the field." While they were in the field, Cain attacked his brother Abel and killed him.

Cain's anger escalated which led to an outward expression of harm. God attempted to intervene by assuring Cain that his inward anger, which was inappropriate, could be mastered and controlled. God said to Cain, "Sin is lurking after you, in fact it is at your doorstep. It desires to devour and destroy you but you have the personal choice to not be mastered by it." God told Cain that he must suppress this inappropriate anger that has gone wild. In other words, God is saying it might be a struggle but you do not have to be mastered by your emotion of anger.

He says to suppress your anger. I want to encourage you to suppress the impulse to retaliate and express your emotions inappropriately. You must suppress the outward expression of anger, which is often rage, but you must release the inward anger over to God. Failure to suppress the outward expression of anger will lead to destructive and ungodly actions and behaviors. And failure to release your inward anger will lead to the destruction of one's self.

What happens when we suppress our anger inward? Suppressed anger can be an underlying cause of anxiety and depression. Anger that is not expressed appropriately can affect thinking and behavior patterns and create a variety of physical problems. Long-term anger has been linked to high blood pressure, heart problems, headaches, skin disorders, and digestive problems.

When we suppress we stop or prohibit, we restrain and keep the anger within instead of letting it go. When we suppress anger, whether that anger is just or unjust, it is like being constipated. Constipation occurs due to one's elimination passage being blocked. It is similar to a dam, where the flow of water is prevented due to a blockage. Eventually, you will be clogged up so much with toxins that your body will become a human trash dump.

The key to mastery over suppressed anger is to do the opposite of suppressing. Instead of suppressing it you must release it. Let your anger go, release it through appropriate means such as venting, counseling, exercise, and most importantly forgiveness. Ultimately, you must **release your anger to God** and allow him to address the legitimate anger.

Release the idea of revenge, and retaliation for this only fuels your anger. Surrender your offender totally over to God, so you are free from the emotional grip of anger.

Whenever you are experiencing sickness in your body, relationships or in general areas of your life, examine yourself to see if you are holding on to anger and unforgiveness. Ask God to help you to hold on to His promise that "vengeance is mine… I will repay says the Lord."

It is important to remember that when you chose not to release your anger to God, you hurt yourself far more than you hurt your offender. In fact, you set yourself up for another debilitating cancer of emotion to take root, which we will examine in the next chapter – unforgiveness.

Do not repay anyone evil for evil. Be careful to do what is right in the eyes of everybody. If it is possible, as far as it depends on you, live at peace with everyone. Do not take revenge, my friends, but leave room for God's wrath, for it is written: 'It is mine to avenge; I will repay,' says the Lord. On the contrary: 'If your enemy is hungry, feed him; if he is thirsty, give him something to drink. In doing this, you will heap burning coals on his head.' Do not be overcome by evil, but overcome evil with good. (Romans 12:17-21)

Affirmation

I am the master of my anger. Love dominates. I am no longer filled with hate. I no longer desire to retaliate out of anger. I chose to retaliate out of love. I am the master of my anger. I release my anger over to God. I release my hurts into the hands of God. God will repay them, God will deal with them. Today I no longer carry the burden to justify myself. I am free from anger because I have released it to God. I am the master of my anger. I am free from anger and it shows, I am consumed with good thoughts, kind thoughts and loving thoughts. I am filled with and expressing good deeds. If my enemy is hungry, I will feed them, if thirsty, I will give them drink, if in my presence I will bless them with peace. I am the master of my anger.

Abridged Affirmation

I am free from anger because I have released it to God. I am the master of my anger. I am free from anger and it shows, I am consumed with good thoughts, kind thoughts and loving thoughts. I am filled with expressing good deeds. If my enemy is hungry I will feed them, if thirsty I will give them drink, if in my presence I will bless them with peace.

Synergy Prayer

Dear Lord,
I thank you that you have equipped me with the spirit
of self-control; I thank you that through you I can
do all things; I thank you that the spirit of hate and
rage is dissolved; and I thank you that I can place my
hurts and destructive emotions into your care. Now
empower me through your grace to express my anger
in a manner that is God-honoring and God-pleasing.
By faith I accept your truth because you said it; and
because you said it, I believe it, even if I can't conceive
it." Amen

Chapter 8

Victory Over Unforgiveness

At the heart of unforgiveness is a strong desire to repay, re-inflict, re-injure, and retaliate against those who hurt you. Isn't it interesting that many of the adverbs that describe the action of those who react to their hurt in a negative manner often begin with the prefix "re-" which means "again." When we repay, re-inflict, re-injure, or retaliate, we again administer the pains, hurts, and wrongs one experiences by passing it on to another. Perhaps we should call it "pay it backwards." The sad reality is that one wrong could live on past a person's lifetime and effect hundreds, even millions, of people because one wrong act was redistributed to another, another, and another. A non-stop, endless cycle of hurt and pain. There has to be a better way. It is no surprise that we live in such an angry and hostile society. Proverbs 17:9 says, "The one who forgives an offense seeks love."

How do we reverse this negative cycle? The opposite side of unforgiveness is forgiveness, where a person relinquishes, releases, and relieves the wrongs, the injustices, the hurts, and the pains inflicted, and turns them over to God to repay. It is God who revenges and redeems the losses and the hurts. Romans 12:19 says, "Do not avenge yourselves , dear friends, but give place to God's wrath, for it is written, "Vengeance is mine, I will repay," says the Lord."

Job having experienced much anguish could easily have allowed anger and bitterness to control him but he coined the words, "I know that my Redeemer lives." (Job 19:25) Webster's Dictionary defines "redeem" in this way: "To free from what distresses or harms, to extricate from or help to overcome something detrimental. To repair, restore, to offset the bad effect."

The word "redeem" first appears in Scripture in connection with Jacob's blessing to his son, Joseph, where the verb is in the present tense: "The angel that redeems me from all evil," Genesis 48:16.

If there is one individual who experienced and understood pain, hurt, betrayal, and injustice, it is Joseph who, after being betrayed by his brothers and sold into slavery, relinquished his injustice to God for redemption. Joseph shifted his focus from man to God. Instead of focusing on the wrong and those who inflicted the wrong, he focused his attention on His redeemer, God.

"As for you, you meant to harm me, but God intended it for a good purpose, so he could preserve the lives of many people, as you can see this day." Genesis 50:20

When we experience hurt it is a natural reflection and innate desire to seek revenge. However, God assures us that He will bring about retribution on our behalf if we put our accusers, abusers, those who afflict us, and those who are our adversaries into his hands. God will, and wants to, handle those who mess with his precious children.

Affirmation

*I know that my Redeemer lives (Job 19:25).
Today I am healed from the spirit of unforgiveness, I
relinquish the pains, hurts, and injustices inflicted upon
me. No longer do I take matters into my own hands,
I choose to surrender my afflicters, accusers, and
assaulters into Your hands.*

*"Do not avenge yourselves, dear friends, but give place
to God's wrath, for it is written, 'Vengeance is mine, I will repay,
says the Lord.'" Romans 12:19-20*

*The things that have been stolen and lost, like my rights,
my respect, my honor, my innocence, are being restored
to me in abundance. I know that my redeemer lives.*

*"So I will restore to you the years that the swarming
locust has eaten, the crawling locust, the consuming locust, and
the chewing locust, my great army which I sent among you. You
shall eat in plenty and be satisfied, and praise the name of the
Lord your God." Joel 2:25-26*

*Today I am rejoicing in my spirit of forgiveness. My
confidence is in God to work on my behalf. He will
repay; he will revenge. He will retaliate. I don't use
my energy, efforts, time, thoughts, or resources toward
redeeming myself. Why? Because it is an act of futility,
for God fights my battles for me.*

*"The Lord will fight for you, you don't have to lift a
finger. 'Vengeance is mine, I will repay,' says the Lord." Exodus
14:25*

*I will not hinder God's intervention. I will allow Him,
and Him alone, to handle my hurts.*

"Do not say, I'll pay you back for this wrong! Wait for the Lord, and He will deliver you." Proverbs 20:22

I choose to pray for and release my enemy, my accuser, afflicter, and assaulter. For my redeemer lives.

"Do not gloat when your enemy falls; when he stumbles, do not let your heart rejoice, or the Lord will see and disapprove and turn his wrath away from him." Proverbs 24:17

Abridged Affirmation

Today I am rejoicing in my spirit of forgiveness. My confidence is in God to work on my behalf. He will repay; he will revenge. He will retaliate. I don't use my energy, efforts, time, thoughts, or resources toward redeeming myself because I know my redeemer lives.

Synergy Prayer

Dear Lord,
I thank you that you are my redeemer, I thank you that no weapon formed against me shall prosper, I thank you that you have promised to repay those who have afflicted me. I thank you that I can put my trust in the fact that you are a just and fair God. Now, Lord please help me to release those who have hurt me because I know that I can't forgive them on my own. So I allow you to express your love for them through me. By faith, I accept this truth because you said it, and because you said it, I believe it, even, if I can't conceive it.

Transformed Through *His* Thoughts

Chapter 9

Victory Over Depression

Depression is another negative emotion that can destroy a person. Consider the prefix "de-", which means from, down or away. It symbolizes moving someone or something in the direction away from the current direction or status. When one departs they move in a different direction. The word down describes the prefix de-. One who is depressed is in a downward emotional state.

The other word we see in depression is "press." According to Webster's Dictionary, press means to act upon through steady pushing or thrusting force exerted in contact; to move by means of pressure.

When you put de with press you get depression; a state of being pressed down, in other words, a heavy load of sadness. A close relative is dejection: a disorder marked by sadness, inactivity, difficulty in thinking and concentration, a significant increase or decrease in appetite and time spent sleeping, feelings of dejection and hopelessness, and sometimes suicidal tendencies, according to Webster.

When life circumstances, events, and experiences become overwhelming, the pressures of life have forced you or pushed you in the opposite direction of joy and happiness. Negative events or circumstances have swung you to the other side of the pendulum. You have been demoted, dejected, and if controlled and ruled by these circumstances you can experience depression.

Once you have departed from that state of joy and happiness, how do you swing back to the other side of the pendulum? How do you effectively return to that state of joy and happiness? Is your only hope to experience a change of life events and circumstances? Certainly that wouldn't hurt the matter. Certainly you would feel better if life's struggles automatically ceased and events became favorable toward you. I sincerely hope that your negative circumstances change, but that is not always possible, or even plausible. While you wait on the Lord for your change, perhaps you would consider changing your perspective, for I believe a person can reverse their emotional state, regardless of circumstances, through a positive frame of mind. Chuck Swindoll put it this way:

The longer I live, the more I realize the impact of attitude on life. Attitude, to me, is more important than facts. It is more important than the past, education, money, than circumstances, than failure, than successes, than what other people think or say or do. It is more important than appearance, giftedness or skill. It will make or break a company... a church... a home. The remarkable thing is we have a choice everyday regarding the attitude we will embrace for that day. We cannot change our past... we cannot change the fact that people will act in a certain way. We cannot change the inevitable. The only thing we can do is play on the one string we have, and that is our attitude. I am convinced that life is 10% what happens to me and 90% of how I

Transformed Through *His* Thoughts

react to it. And so it is with you... we are in charge of our attitudes.

In the book of Lamentations, there is a literal depiction of Jeremiah crying out in grief. However, in this book of sorrows, a nugget of gold is found in Lamentation 3:19-24: "Just thinking about my impoverished and homeless condition is bitter poison. When I continually think about this, I become emotionally depressed. **But this I call to mind**, therefore I have hope. The Lord's many kindness never cease, for his great compassion never comes to an end. They are renewed every morning, your faithfulness is abundant! I said to myself, 'The Lord is the portion of my inheritance; therefore, I will put my hope in him.' "

What a joyous declaration and an amazing redirection of thought. The writer of this book started out in a state of emotional turmoil but by the end of verse 24 he had a complete turnaround. Why the immediate change? Was it circumstance? Obviously not, but it was a change of perspective. The author reasoned in his mind that God's love for him never ceases even if he is not aware of this love.

In the physical realm, the writer encouraged himself with the autosuggestion, "The Lord is the **portion of my inheritance.**" (verse 24) This is a beautiful example of how we have to get our minds unstuck from the gutter. When life throws negative circumstances our way, it is a natural tendency to sink into a melancholy state. But we must learn to encourage ourselves in the Lord, by recalling his wonderful truths and promises.

Paul said in Philippians 4:8 "Finally brothers and sisters, whatever is true, whatever is worthy of respect, whatever is just, whatever is pure, whatever is lovely, whatever is commendable, if something is excellent or praiseworthy, think about these things."

In Acts 16, Paul and Silas cast out the evil spirit in a

slave-girl who was bringing much profit through her fortune telling. As a result, it caused uproar:

And the crowd rose up together against them, and the chief magistrates tore their robes off them, and proceeded to order them to be beaten with rods. And when they had inflicted many blows upon them, they threw them into prison, commanding the jailer to guard them securely; and he, having received such a command, threw them into the inner prison, and fastened their feet in the stocks. (vs 25) But about midnight Paul and Silas were praying and singing hymns of praise to God, and the prisoners were listening to them; and suddenly there came a great earthquake, so that the foundations of the prison house were shaken; and immediately all the doors were opened, and everyone's chains were unfastened.

What a vivid illustration, that joy does not have to be associated with positive circumstances and events. Paul and Silas, in spite of negative and harsh surroundings, shifted the pendulum of sadness and pain to joy. *What was the major shift, their circumstance or their perspectives regarding the circumstance?* Actually, nothing had changed, they were still locked up and suffering from the pain of their wounds. In their down state they looked upward to God and began to praise Him and pray to Him. Wow, I would love to have a copy of that prayer because whatever they prayed it was so powerful that not only did it unleash them, but the entire prison ward was released from the chains that bound them.

Although a copy of the prayer is not supplied in the text, what is supplied provides ample insight into how you can transform a depressed state into a joyous state. They rose above their circumstances. They made a conscience decision and choice to praise God regardless of their present state. They took charge of their emotions and redirected them by consciously turning their thoughts toward their great God. They *redirected* their perspective by **singing hymns of praise**.

In the book of Ephesians, Paul exhorts us on how to

                                                    Transformed Through *His* Thoughts

walk in the spirit. He says do not get drunk or intoxicated with wine, but to be intoxicated in the spirit. Intoxication causes you to do things you normally would not do. A person drunk on wine will speak and act bolder and can often engage in uncivilized behavior. But a person intoxicated in the spirit will defy human circumstances and react in ways that cause them to speak and act wisely and model Christ-like behavior.

How does one get drunk in The Spirit? Ephesians 5:18-20 states:

And do not get drunk with wine, which is debauchery, but be filled by the Spirit, speaking to one another in psalms, hymns, and spiritual songs, singing and making music in your hearts to the Lord.

In order to display a spirit-controlled life, one should incorporate Psalms, hymns, and spiritual songs, singing and making melody to the Lord in your heart. **Shift your focus from your surroundings to God's word and spiritual music that can uplift your spirit and redirect your focus.**

Then, verse 20 says to have an attitude of gratitude, "Always giving thanks for all things." Learn the habit of praising God for the good and the bad, for He is still in control, and if He allowed it, He can handle it! Surely, if he brought you to it, He can get you through it. If God allowed the circumstance which seems frustrating, difficult, uneasy, emotionally draining, causing your spirituality to wan and your physical demeanor to appear as if you are insane, He can help you overcome it. It is at these times, which are so crucial and pivotal, that you must make the emotional shift. But it is hard, unnatural, and against the grain and natural flow of your emotional current. In a sense, it is like swimming upstream.

Managing your emotional state is similar to the Alaskan salmon when it swims upstream against rugged rapids, leaping over rocky waterfalls, traversing fish ladders, avoiding fisherman nets and hooks, and staying clear of hungry bears. Why do the salmon bother with this great struggle? It is their natural instinct to be concerned with productivity versus comfort. Productivity is better known as reproduction. The spawning adult realizes that in order to produce life they must struggle upstream to create a safe environment for the salmon eggs to hatch. These creatures understand, either consciously or unconsciously, that struggle, difficulty, and pain are often the passage to life. Jesus, himself said, "…for the joy set before me, I endured the cross." In other words it was the cross (the upstream battle) that gave Jesus His joy and the joy of those who believe.

This emotional shift is not about feelings. Your feelings will not motivate, encourage, or rev your spirit up with excitement so that you act with joy because everything around you produces zero joy. If the circumstances were favorable; i.e. you received a raise, purchased a house, your relationship with your spouse or significant other is heaven-like, your children are saints and making straight A's, then joy would literally knock you over like an excited overgrown dog when you come home after being gone all day.

What I am proposing is to celebrate the positive circumstances prior to their arrival. To rejoice about the good times to come while still in the midst of the bad times. Now, this takes faith! "Now, faith is the substance of things hope for and the evidence of things **not seen**." (Hebrews 11:1)

James said it best in James 1:2-4: "Consider it all joy, my brethren, when you encounter various trials." Why should I count it all joy? Because the testing of your faith produces endurance. And what good is endurance? James continues, "And let endurance have its perfect result, **that you may be perfect and complete, lacking nothing.**"

The role of endurance is that God wants to conform us to be like Christ. Christ endured the cross for the joy that was set before him. The trials of life sharpen us, but the endurance allows us to remain in the fight of faith. "So do not grow weary in well doing or in your time of undoing for in due season if we can endure we will become like Christ. For He who began a good work in you will complete it." (Phil 1:6)

I believe that endurance is one of the major ingredients of being a faithful follower of Christ. For, it is not how we start but how we finish the race. "The race is not given to the swift but to those who endure." What makes a good spouse? One who can endure the ups and downs of marriage. What makes one a good student? One who can endure the rigorous demands of a doctoral program. What makes a good employee? One who can endure the difficult times on the job. What makes one a great distant runner? Those who may not be the fastest, but who can consistently keep the pace over an extended period of time.

Let us return to the story of Joseph (Genesis, chapters 37-50), which we briefly encountered in Chapter 8. In a dream, Joseph saw the place of greatness that God would eventually take him to, but he met with opposition when his brothers ridiculed him and sold him into slavery. His world went from great to gloom, from delight to doom, from enjoyment to imprisonment. Yet, Joseph in Genesis 50:20 said, "As for you, you meant to harm me, but God intended it for a good purpose, so he could preserve the lives of many people, as you can see this day." Joseph understood that his trials were used by God to create good for himself but also for the people of Israel. Note, being sold into slavery and later thrown into prison unjustly were circumstances so difficult many could not bear them, but those circumstances turned out for the good, and not just for Joseph, but for two nations. In the end, Joseph was a refined and changed man, fully used by God, as a result of his patient endurance in his trials.

I encourage you to endure your difficult days because better days are coming. But more wonderful than the hope of better days is the truth that we will become better people and God will have his perfect way. Decide today to fast-forward your emotions to your breakthrough and deliverance while you are going through your bondage of emotional frustration. Praise God in the midst of your bondage as Paul and Silas did in prison.

Experience deliverance emotionally while you wait on the Lord to work out your circumstance.

Affirmation

I am the master of my emotions. I will control my spirit and become greater than a mighty warrior (Proverbs 16:32). For when I control my spirit and emotions there will be nothing else I cannot control. When I feel down I will shift my emotions upward. I will do this by focusing my mind on things that are pure, just, holy, good, righteous, lovely, excellent and praiseworthy. When my mind craves the self-entertainment of self-pity due to my unfavorable situations, I will fast-forward my emotions to a place of joy, since God will ultimately produce good from my trials, and He is completing in me His perfect work. I am master of my downward state, and today, regardless of my emotional, relational, financial, occupational or personal state, I choose to be in an upward state of happiness and joy.

I am the master over my depression. I will not allow my unfavorable life events, people, circumstances or myself to bring me down. I choose to find God in every life event. Since God is there, all will be good.

I am the master over my depression. Even though I may walk through the valley of the shadow of death, I will fear nothing for God is with me. He is my guide, my shield, and protector. I shall not want because I know my Shepard will watch over me.(Psalm 23) I choose today to shift my downward state to an upward state of joy and happiness because I believe God will work all things eventually into His good and my favor. For the Lord has plans to prosper me and not to harm me. (Jeremiah 29:11)

Abridged Affirmation

I am the master over my depression. Even though I may walk through the valley of the shadow of death, I will fear nothing for God is with me. He is my guide, my shield, and my protector. I shall not want because I know my Shepard will watch over me. I choose today to shift my downward state to an upward state of joy and happiness because I believe God will work all things eventually into His good and my favor.

Synergy Prayer:

Dear Lord,
I thank you that you promised to be with me as I walk through the valley and lows of life. I thank you that you are capable of turning my midnight into daylight. I thank you that you promised not to put more on me than I can bear. I thank you that you have given me your holy spirit to intercede, when I am so burdened that I can't even begin to share my deep despair. I thank you that through my trails you are making me more like you. Now, by faith I accept this truth because you said it, and because you said it, I believe it, even if I can't conceive it. Amen

Chapter 10

Victory over Fear

Fear is one of the most detrimental emotions known to mankind. It has affected trillions of people from every culture, in every city, in every country. It has been around since the beginning of time, when Satan used fear (the fear of losing out on something better) to manipulate Eve. The spirit of fear is a master at spreading its deadly effect on people, usually without using any force. It is one of the major tools of Satan to prevent God's people from walking in a life of faith.

Fear operates with three distinct characteristics:

1. It causes paralysis
2. It often stems from exaggeration or exaggerated perception
3. It is fueled by uncertainty and the unknown

Paralysis

The most prominent characteristic of fear is that it causes paralysis, whether emotional or physical. It keeps people from moving toward their objectives, goals, dreams, and visions. Fear is not a physical force, but a mental force stronger than all the Mr. Universes throughout history combined. Could you imagine trying to penetrate through a wall that consisted of a line of all the Mr. Universes? Ronnie Coleman, Arnold Schwarzenegger, etc., and you have to break through it? Most of you would say, "No way! I would not even try." Fear is that wall of Mr. Universes in your mind that causes you to be immobilized. But are those obstacles really muscle-bound giants?

Exaggeration
Fear is a game, a game of exaggeration. In our minds, we all tend to exaggerate the things we fear, so we never act. We create a giant, a Mr. Universe, out of a midget and paint a figment in our minds that causes us to live in a bind, caught between desire to act and fear of action. But when you address your fear, you automatically address your propensity to procrastinate. For procrastination, after all, often disguises fear of action.

Fear of the Unknown
The third element of fear also can be a cause of procrastination. The very idea of never having travelled through a certain experience, can keep you from ever doing it. Unfamiliar events, circumstances and even people can be scary. But once you have traveled down a path, the fear and timidity lessen because now you have familiarity. The sad reality is that if we never venture out, we will always remain stuck in the same place. We will never experience new horizons, opportunities, adventures, people or places. We will never explore the vast and enormous opportunities in life. We will never become all that God has ordained us to be, unless we learn to control fear.

Taming the Beast
The more you step out in spite of what fear is telling

		Transformed Through *His* Thoughts

you, the quicker the mental chains of fear will be broken. Do the thing that you are afraid and timid about, and the fear and timidity will disappear.

Consider my definition of fear: Fear is when one is **F**ocused **E**xclusively on **A**ffirming **R**everence toward a person, place, thing, activity, or situation. Granted, the reverence is unrealistic and negative, but it is that very act of giving undue reverence toward a person, place, thing, activity or situation that is most crucial.

The goal to overcoming fear is mobilization – to become actively involved in doing those things that will enable you to explore and enjoy enormous opportunities in life. The key ingredient needed to push you into mobilization is **courage**. Courage is mental or moral strength to venture, persevere, and withstand danger, fear, or difficulty according to Webster's Collegiate Dictionary.

It is very interesting to me that within the word courage we find **rage**. Now, rage is normally associated with something that should be in a cage, an animal or person with violent and uncontrolled anger. Yet rage can also mean intense feelings or passion. An intense feeling or passion is very hard to keep immobilized. The origin of the word courage in Old French is corage, from Latin "cor" meaning heart. So, courage is an intensely passionate heart that, with an indomitable spirit, faces challenges.

There is a fear, however, that is a holy fear. Awe, perhaps, is a better word in today's vernacular. But in this fear, we find the very opposite of what the spirit of fear gives us. *In the **fear** of the Lord, one has a strong **confidence**.* "He who fears the LORD has a secure fortress, and for his children it will be a refuge." Proverbs 14:26

Courage is facing your fear in spite of the unknown. Yet, with God on your side you can be confident that He is with you and that He knows the unknown. So that whatever you face, from a mountain top experience to a Death Valley journey, God is your shield and protector. (Psalm 23)

Joshua can attest to this courage in spite of the unknown. God spoke to him, as recorded in Joshua 1:5-9:

*No one will be able to stand up against you all the days of your life. As I was with Moses, so I will be with you; I will never leave you nor forsake you. 'Be strong and **courageous**, because you will lead these people to inherit the land I swore to their forefathers to give them. Be strong and **very courageous**. Be careful to obey all the law my servant Moses gave you; do not turn from it to the right or to the left, that you may be successful wherever you go. Do not let this Book of the Law depart from your mouth; meditate on it day and night, so that you may be careful to do everything written in it. Then you will be prosperous and successful. Have I not commanded you? Be strong and **courageous**. Do not be terrified; do not be discouraged, for the LORD your God will be with you wherever you go.'*

There are three principles within this passage that are reinforced:

1. Know I am with you in your journey.
2. Be strong and courageous in your journey.
3. Prioritize and fulfill my ways in your journey.

If you do steps one through three, then you will be successful. (Josh 1:5-8)

God tells Joshua twice that He will be with him and that he will not fail or forsake him. But he tells Joshua three times to be strong and very courageous. God is saying to Joshua, and to you, do not allow your fears to paralyze you and cause you to become immobilized.

I believe that God emphasizes being strong and courageous because these attributes are directly related to preventing the children of Israel from making the same mistake as when they were about to take the Promised Land – they were gripped with fear, uncertainty, and discouragement. Look at the word "discourage," the direct opposite of courage. To discourage, according to Encarta dictionary, is to prevent something from happening by making it more difficult or unpleasant. To make somebody feel less motivated, confident, or optimistic." The prefix 'dis' means away, not, or negative. Therefore, dis/courage is to be away from courage. A prime example of discouragement can be seen in the attitude and emotional state of the Children of Israel. After their many years of great oppression by the Egyptians they had lost all hope and any motivation. In fact, this apparently was a flaw in the character of the children of Israel for, as they were exiting Egypt, fear almost kept them from freedom. In Exodus 13:17-18, we see how God intervened to help the Israelites with their enormous fear. When Pharaoh let the Israelites go, he led them through the scenic route because of their lack of faith and debilitating fears. The Bible says He did this so they would not change their minds and return to Egypt when they experienced opposition.

Every opposition you face requires courage and bravery. There is no such thing as easy opposition. In fact the greater the opposition, the greater your reward when you face it.

Perhaps at times, you, like the Israelites, have exaggerated fear. Their fear was so enlarged that they wanted to remain as slaves in Egypt versus experiencing the great freedom God had for them and becoming owners and possessors themselves. Their fear had caused them to become complacent, (Exodus 14:10-12) but Moses encouraged the people to stop fearing and face their opposition. Lock eyes and lock horns with your opponent; stop giving your ground away. (Exodus 14:13-15)

Why could Moses give this charge? Because he knew God would be with them. "The Lord will fight for you, and you can be still." (verse 14) I believe this stillness is standing firm on the promises of God and not being moved by our emotions.

Where there is inner peace and rest there is confidence. Where there is confidence, one can move forward in faith. (Exodus 14:15)

When Moses tells his people to move forward, they are going into the Red Sea without any life-saving gear. When we move forward in faith and courage, we do not know what's on the other side! That is why we call the action faith. But you can never experience the other side if you remain paralyzed by fear.

God tells Joshua in Joshua 1:5-8 to move forward and possess the land He has already prepared for them, but He warns Joshua that strength and bravery will be necessary for obedience. Faith is needed for obedience because it is taking God at His word, even if we cannot see it or understand it. Faith takes enormous courage. What we see in this awesome passage is that faith and courage were necessary to take what already belonged to the children of Israel. (Joshua 2:9-11)

In order for us to conquer in life we must conquer our fear first. Fear leads to procrastination, but courageous faith leads to productivity and possession.

"THE GREATER THE OPPOSITION, THE GREATER THE REWARD WHEN YOU FACE IT."   *--Guy Earle*

"FEAR CAUSES APPREHENSION, APPREHENSION CAUSES A LACK OF ATTENTION, AND A LACK OF ATTENTION WILL LEAD TO MANY PREVENTIONS."
--Guy Earle

"FAITH ON THE OTHER HAND IS ASSURANCE. ASSURANCE IN GOD LEADS TO INSURANCE IN LIFE. ONE WHO IS INSURED CAN LIVE WITH ABANDOMENT."
--Guy Earle

   Transformed Through *His* Thoughts

What Appears is Not Always So

In I Samuel 17, David faces the gigantic Goliath. Goliath is a champion; perhaps we could call him Goliath the Gladiator. Everything about Goliath was gargantuan. His armor consisted of a bronze helmet, bronze body armor, bronze shin guards, a bronze javelin, and a spear with an iron point, which alone weighed 15 pounds. It is estimated that Goliath's body armor weighed close to 200 pounds or more.

Imagine that David, a young teen of about 14, most likely didn't weigh anywhere near 200 pounds, and if he wore even an average adult's armor he surely wouldn't be too swift. One thing we do know is that David was not favored to win this fight. From a human perspective, everything appeared as if this were a really bad deal for Israel. David didn't have on the proper gear to protect himself, for it was too cumbersome. (1 Samuel 17:38) I am sure the people were saying, "We might as well surrender now, for Goliath will demolish David – it isn't even a fair contest."

But what David did possess could not be measured by appearance. David had a courageous heart, one that was unafraid, unashamed and unabashed to stand up and fight for the name of his God and his people.

David said to Saul, *'Let no one lose heart on account of this Philistine; your servant will go and fight him.' Saul replied, 'You are not able to go out against this Philistine and fight him; you are only a boy, and he has been a fighting man from his youth.' But David said to Saul, 'Your servant has been keeping his father's sheep. When a lion or a bear came and carried off a sheep from the flock, I went after it, struck it and rescued the sheep from its mouth. When it turned on me, I seized it by its jaw, struck it and killed it. Your servant has killed both the lion and the bear; this uncircumcised Philistine will be like one of them, because he has defied the armies of the living God. The LORD who delivered me from the paw of the lion and the paw of the bear will deliver me from the hand of this Philistine.' Saul said to David, 'Go, and the LORD be with you.'* (1 Samuel 17:32-37)

David was saying to Saul, don't allow the people to fear. Literally he said don't let them have a lack of courage. For I am here to save the day. Can you imagine Saul perhaps thinking, "Who is this over confident lad?"

Verse 33 is crucial. Saul said, in effect, "Ok that is all nice but you would be committing suicide. You can't fight this giant. You're a boy, and he is a seasoned and trained ultimate fighter." Most of us at that time would think perhaps Saul was right and we'd leave it alone. David, not shaken by the doubt in Saul, looked him straight in the eyes with confidence and says, "I am a lion and bear slayer. As a shepherd, if a lion or bear takes one of my sheep I go after it, I hunt it down and strike it down until it puts my sheep down. If it rises up against me I would grab it by the jaws, strike it, and kill it." That is courage and conviction.

One thing I have observed about David is that he was very precise. He wasn't consumed by fear or doubt. He knew he could do the job. His assurance was so strong, in fact, that he persuaded Saul to let him fight this beast of a giant. Now, there is one key phrase I want to highlight: "The Lord who delivered me from the lion and the bear will also deliver me from the hand of this Philistine!"

David was saying, "I can be strong and very courageous because I know the Lord is with me. I know that He can give me success; *I am not looking at the size of the gargantuan giant, but I am focused on my gargantuan* God." Face your giant. Don't become paralyzed by focusing on the size of your giant but shift your focus to how big, awesome, and powerful your God is.

It is fascinating to me that David's courage was backed by a calculated method of attack. Let's observe how he would deal with his opposition, whether man or beast.

When David would go retrieve the sheep from the vicious lion or bear, he did it with precision and laser-beam

    Transformed Through *His* Thoughts

focus, like a skilled assassin. He didn't go with enthusiasm only, but he also had a practiced method for slaying his enemy.

I Samuel 17:35 says, *"I would go out after it, strike it down, and rescue the sheep from its mouth, if it rose up against me, I would grab it by its jaw, strike it, and kill it."* David would first grab the beast by the jaw. Upon quick reading, this phrase can easily be over looked, but to attack the jaws is to go after the jugular. The jugular is the most vital or vulnerable part of a living thing. David was going after the kill; he wasn't trying to get this large cat or oversized teddy bear to retreat. No, his aim and focus was to defeat. With intense focus and unadulterated courage, he went for the most deadly point of his opponent, the jaws. If the jaws had latched onto David, it would be the end of him. Most people would try to avoid the jaws for this reason, but consider this: if you control the jaws, you control the beast. James 3:3, says that the bridle controls the entire body of the horse. For if you can control the head you can control the entire body.

Occasionally, I enjoy the adventurous animal shows on television. When the host is trying to catch a wild animal, he almost always seeks to go after the head. If the deadly snake's head and jaws are controlled, it cannot harm the one who catches it.

My point is that being controlled by fear does not allow one to go after the deadly jaws of a beast. In fact, when you are controlled by fear, the jaws of the beast control you. But being controlled by courageous faith gives you an offensive, rather than defensive, mindset. Now you are on the attack. What are you going after with unbridled faith, focus, and fervor?

YOUR FOCUS WILL DETERMINE WHETHER YOU SINK IN CIRCUMSTANCES OR WALK IN FAITH

You can either focus on fear or focus your faith on God. You can be preoccupied with your surroundings, or you can be preoccupied with the strength of your God. In Matthew 8:23-27,

Jesus and the disciples were in the boat on the sea and a great storm appeared to be overtaking them. In a state of panic, the frightened disciples woke Jesus and cried, "Lord save us. We are about to die!" Fear often causes people to predict an unfavorable future. Now, certainly the circumstances were bleak, but they had forgotten who was in the boat with them. The first thing Jesus said to them was "Why are you cowardly, you people of little faith? Why are you so timid, fearful and uncourageous? Where is your unshakable faith?" Then Jesus commanded the winds and the sea to be still and the tumultuous waves and winds became calm.

The disciples witnessed the truth that if Jesus were with them, there was no storm to big for Him to subdue. The reason we as believers can be courageous is because God has promised that He will never leave us nor forsake us.

Another example of how your focus will cause you either to sink in circumstances or walk in faith is seen in Matthew 14:22-31. In this passage Jesus sends off the disciples into the boat for a quick get away before he dismissed the crowds – not unlike a situation where people leave the game early to beat the rush at a sporting event or, sadly, even church. Jesus, after dismissing the crowds, goes to the mountain to pray. Meanwhile, the disciples are in a storm at sea. Sometime between 3 a.m. – 6 a.m., Jesus began walking on top of the sea, toward the disciples' boat. In the dark and the mist, the disciples didn't recognize Jesus and thought he was a ghost. They cried out in terror. Now, please let's not be too quick to judge, for I know that if I saw someone walking on water in the midst of turbulent waves, I would be frightened myself. My heart would begin to race and if it weren't for the confines of the boat, I would most likely run. Yet, the disciples were captive to the boat and water, and they could only wait to see who or what this strange apparition is. Jesus spoke up and said, "Have courage! It is I, don't be afraid."

The scene that takes place next is one of the most amazing and awe-inspiring miracles in the Bible. After Jesus spoke, Peter suddenly acted like he just heard a motivational message from Zig Zigglar. He spoke up with this out-of-the-box, out-of-the-ordinary request, "Order me to come to you on the water, if it is really you." Jesus said one word, "Come!"

When is the last time we asked God for an out-of-the-box, out-of-the-ordinary request, something that has never been done or witnessed by mankind? I assure you prior to meeting Jesus and being on the multiple fishing outings, the disciples had never seen a human being walk on water.

But when Jesus called to him, Peter got out of the boat and walked on the water, heading toward Jesus. Wow! What a sight! What a bold request, a bold reaction on Peter's part, but most importantly, what an out-of-this-world result! Peter got out of the boat and he began to actually walk on the water. *The great request was accompanied by great courage and faith, which produced an extraordinary result.* Unfortunately, however, this extraordinary result was short lived. Why? The text gives two reasons why Peter sank. The first destroyer of courage and faith is to allow yourself to become preoccupied with what the human eye sees. "Peter saw the strong wind," the Bible tells us. Peter lost focus. He walked toward Jesus at first, so his focus was on the Savior. He locked eyes with Jesus because he couldn't have walked toward him if he hadn't known where he was. But when Peter took his focus off of Jesus and began to examine the storm, he became afraid.

This leads to the second destroyer of courage and faith – allowing yourself to become preoccupied with fear. Being preoccupied with what you see and with what you fear go hand-in-hand. Immediately, when Peter lost focus and courage, he began to sink. Now if you want to know the sure formula to sinking in life, then simply focus on the enormous obstacles in your life and become overly fearful due to those perceived mountains. Jesus, being the life-saver, rescued Peter. But He was obviously disappointed, because He said, "You of little faith, why did you doubt?" Jesus so wanted Peter to show indomitable faith in the face of insurmountable obstacles.

Remember: Fear is when one is **F**ocused **E**xclusively on **A**ffirming **R**everence toward a person, place, thing, activity, or situation. It is unrealistic reverence toward someone or something. In this case, Peter focused his reverence on the sea, rather than on Jesus.

Faith, on the other hand, is **F**ocused on **A**nticipating deliverance **I**nspite of **T**roublesome obstacles and **H**ellish circumstances.

Faith is a laser-beam focus on the attributes, incredible power, terrific, and hell-defeating strength of our God.   2 Timothy 1:7 says, "For God did not give us a spirit of fear but of power and love and self-control."

Affirmation

I no longer am focused exclusively on affirming unrealistic reverence toward a person, place, thing, activity, or situation. I am focused exclusively on affirming reverence to my God who is able to do exceedingly, abundantly above all I ask or think. I walk in courageous faith, not controlled by figments of my imagination created by fear. I am walking in my ABC's: **A**ssurance, **B**oldness, and **C**onfidence. For if God is for me, who can be against me? I am actively pursuing those things that have caused me to shrink back in a state of complacency. I am fully engaged and focused on my obstacles and opposition. I am strong and very courageous, for my fear has disappeared because my faith is focused on my great, awesome and powerful God. When all odds are against me, I will rejoice because victory rests not in my hands, but in the hands of my God. "A horse I prepared for the day of battle, but the victory is from the Lord." (Proverbs 21:31) I fear no more, because at my core I have put my trust and faith in God and not in what I see. I am the master over my fear.

Abridged Affirmation

I am actively pursuing those things that have caused me to shrink back in a state of complacency. I am fully engaged and focused on my obstacles and opposition. I am strong and very courageous, for my fear has disappeared because my faith is focused on my great, awesome and powerful God.

Synergy Prayer

Dear Lord,
I Thank you that you have not given me a spirit of fear but a spirit of power, love and self-control. I thank you that since you are for me I need not fear anyone or anything. I thank you that with faith in you I can move mountains and overcome obstacles. I thank you that you are a God with no limitations and that there is nothing too hard for you. Therefore, by faith I accept this truth because you said it; and because you said it, I believe it, even if I can't conceive it. Amen

Chapter 11

Victory Over Impatience

Patience is bearing pains or trials calmly or without complaint.   Forbearance under strain, steadfast despite opposition. – Merriam Webster

You can wait on God or choose to move without God. Choosing the latter will lead to exhaustion. Choosing to wait on God will allow you to exhale. We all have areas where we are waiting on God to come through on:
- Career
- Dreams
- Finances
- Relationships

The challenge is to wait, while being patient and learning to enjoy the journey toward our destination. Many of us are like little kids who ask questions incessantly on a road trip. Are we there yet? What time is it? How much longer?

The acronym W.A.I.T. can supply you with a formula so you can enjoy and maximize your journey while you wait for

God's provision.

Work your field

Sometimes you can get so excited about where you are going that you lose focus of where you are. Learn to live fully in the present.

Often we want a promotion, and we aspire for the best. However, there is one key element to any aspiration. Before we seek to move to a different position in life, we must first make sure we have done the needed work within our own soul. Perhaps God has you in a holding pattern until you are ready for your promotion.

1. **Grow more:**
   *My dear brothers, take note of this: Everyone should be quick to listen, slow to speak and slow to become angry, for man's anger does not bring about the righteous life that God desires. Therefore, get rid of all moral filth and the evil that is so prevalent and humbly accept the word planted in you, which can save you. Do not merely listen to the word, and so deceive yourselves. Do what it says. **Anyone who listens to the word but does not do what it says is like a man who looks at his face in a mirror and, after looking at himself, goes away and immediately forgets what he looks like. But the man who looks intently into the perfect law that gives freedom, and continues to do this, not forgetting what he has heard, but doing it—he will be blessed in what he does.** If anyone considers himself religious and yet does not keep a tight rein on his tongue, he deceives himself and his religion is worthless. Religion that God our Father accepts as pure and faultless is this: to look after orphans and widows in their distress and to keep oneself from being polluted by the world." James 1:19-27*

  Transformed Through *His* Thoughts

'know thyself'! Be willing to evaluate your own life to determine traits and flaws that might hinder your personal growth as you journey toward your destination.

2. Prepare more
"Finish your outdoor work and get your fields ready; after that, build your house." Proverbs 24:27

Act as if "that which is not, already is".
Begin to walk as if what you believe God is calling you toward is already there.

"As it is written: 'I have made you a father of many nations.' He is our father in the sight of God, in whom he believed—the God who gives life to the dead and calls things that are not as though they were. Against all hope, Abraham in hope believed and so became the father of many nations, just as it had been said to him, 'So shall your offspring be.'" Romans 4:17-18

Ignite speed through constant cultivation
To cultivate is to grow or tend…to foster and create the environment for growth through proper nurturing.

1. God propels prepared people
"He who goes out weeping, carrying seed to sow, will return with songs of joy, carrying sheaves with him." Psalm 126:6

"Let us not become weary in doing good, for at the proper time we will reap a harvest if we do not give up." Galatians 6:9

Ask yourself the question, how much time and energy have I put into my desired goal? What can I do daily to prepare, assist and accelerate me in the process of achieving my objective?

Time – at the appointed time, fulfillment will come

God is ultimately in control. After you have done all you can—tilled, toiled, planted, and watered, wait for God to give you the increase!

"Oh, the depth of the riches of the wisdom and knowledge of God! How unsearchable his judgments, and his paths beyond tracing out! 'Who has known the mind of the Lord? Or who has been his counselor? Who has ever given to God, that God should repay him?' For from him and through him and to him are all things. To him be the glory forever! Amen," Romans 11:33-36.

"....and having done all you can do, stand!"
Ephesians 6:13

The key to overcoming impatience is to incorporate self-control over one's emotion and to comprehend that God is sovereign. The word sovereign has the word "reign" in it because God is the supreme ruler over everyone and everything. He is truly the King of the jungle.

If we really understood at our core that God is the King and Ruler over all, then we would not panic, worry or become overly anxious. Perhaps we respond in life with panic, worry and anxiety because we don't feel we have control. It is natural to want to be in control, and when control is lost our, emotions erupt like a volcano.

Have you ever noticed how much physical effort your body puts out when you are in a state of impatience? The heart races, your emotional temperature rises, your stomach rumbles, every part of your body accelerates to a higher speed…you talk faster and louder, you can't stay still, your thoughts spiral out of control, your feet begin to tap, your hands begin to fidget, and the emotions of anger, fear, and rage begin to rise. Wow! Talk about a workout! But unlike a normal workout, this is A workout that depletes and tears down your emotional well-being.

The key to victory over impatience is learning to quiet your inner self with all its emotions and feelings, to be still and know that God is God, to be calm, cool and collected – in a nutshell to display a spirit of equanimity in the midst of the storms of life.

The Ray Boltz' song, "The Anchor Holds" beautifully depicts how we can face life and all its challenges when we are holding to the Anchor of our souls:

I have journeyed through the long dark night
out on the open sea by faith alone, sight unknown,
and yet his eyes were watching me.

The anchor holds though the ship is battered the anchor
holds though the sails are torn I have fallen on my knees
as I faced the raging seas the anchor holds in spite of the
storm.

When your anchor is in the Lord, you become very stable in whatever circumstances you encounter. You are like a ship whose anchor prevents it from being carried away by every little wind or current, not to mention every huge wave. Allow your soul to become anchored in the Lord and the negative or positive currents of life will not sweep you away. However, when you allow your faith to wane, you become like the wave of the sea, blown and tossed around by the wind. James describes this person as a double-minded individual unstable in all their ways, a person should not expect to receive anything from the Lord. (James 1:6-8) It is through faith that we please God, and when we honor Him with our faith, He honors us.

Instead of becoming overly moved by situations, resolve to heed the wisdom of Isaiah 30:15, "The Sovereign Lord, the

Holy One of Israel says, 'Only in returning to me and waiting for me will you be saved. In quietness and confidence is your strength, but you would have none of it.'" The phrase "in quietness and confidence is your strength" is a powerful concept. It is a tranquil and quiet spirit that fosters strength. But an uptight, uneasy, unbalanced emotional state literlly drains your spiritual, mental, and physical strength away.

Patience only comes when one is fully at peace in the present. Eckhart Tolle, in The Power of Now highlights this very concept. He enlightens us that we don't know how to be fulfilled in the present moment. So when one learns to have a deep serenity and stillness in the now, it will produce far more joy and benefit than, a frantic unaware soul. (Eckhart, 1999.)

Be still and know that God can guide you to your destination if you are willing to take heed of his "road" signs. For today, "A person plans his course, but the lord directs his steps" Proverbs 16:9.

Affirmations

Today I am the master of my emotions. "Weak is he who permits his thoughts to control his actions; strong is he who forces his actions to control his thoughts." Today I will master my emotions.

I recognize and identify the mystery of moods in all mankind, and in me. From this moment on, I am prepared to control whatever personality awakes in me each day. I will master my moods through positive action and when I master my moods, I will control my destiny.

"He who controls his spirit is greater than he who takes a city." Proverbs 16:32

Self-mastery is greater than any other feat. For when I control myself, I suddenly comprehend that there is nothing I cannot conquer.

God in His unlimited power granted me the task to subdue the earth, but in order to control the world I must first subdue the beast in me. Today I am master of my emotions. Today I have conquered my spirit. Today I take captive all thoughts, feelings, impulses, desires and actions that destroy, and I replace those negative components with thoughts, feelings, impulses, desires and actions, which produce life. I am master of my emotions.

I am calm, even-tempered, relaxed, not flustered. I am master of my emotions. As Jesus spoke peace to the storm so I, too, speak peace over the winds, storms, and rains in my life. Even if the storms keep raging. I am experiencing peace on the inside. Because of the peace of God, which passes all understanding, shall keep my heart and mind through Christ Jesus (Philippians 4:7).

I speak peace over my emotions, peace be still (insert your name), be still. Be still and know that God is God. He is in control; I therefore relinquish all control.

Isaiah 26:3-4

"Thou wilt keep him in perfect peace, whose mind is stayed on thee."

I alter my thinking from my surroundings, circumstances, frustrations, and disappointments. And I shift them to God's greatness, His power, His might, His sovereignty, His will and His way. Peace, be still! Negative emotions once easily revealed have been locked up and sealed.

Thank You, God, for speaking peace over my will. I choose today to be still!

Abridged Affirmation

Today I am the master of my emotions. I am calm, even-tempered, relaxed, not flustered. I am master of my emotions. As Jesus spoke peace to the storm so I, too, speak peace over the winds, storms, and rains in my life. Even if the storms keep raging, I am experiencing peace on the inside. Because the peace of God, which passes all understanding, shall keep my heart and mind through Christ Jesus.

Synergy Prayer

Dear Lord,
I thank you that you have promised that through prayer and gratitude the peace of God will guard my emotions and my mind. I thank you that you have the capacity to calm the raging storms in my life. I thank you that you have promised never to leave me nor forsake me. I thank you that you can keep me in perfect peace if I keep my mind on you. I thank you Lord that you told me I don't have to be anxious over any matter. Therefore, by faith I accept this truth because you said it, and because you said it, I believe it, even if I can't conceive it. Amen

Chapter 12

Victory Over Poverty

Poverty Is a State of Lack.

The Bible says, the poor will always be among us. (Deuteronomy 15:11) But the question is: Does it have to be so? In some cases yes, the country's culture and customs foster a state of lack. Yet, in other instances, the answer is decidedly no. Bad choices, lack of planning, greed and get-rich-quick schemes foster poverty. Both causes lead to the same result, but poverty does not have to be the plight of so many.

Poverty is a state of mind.

To be rich, one doesn't have to possess riches. Some of the most prosperous folks are those with an abundance of health, great and meaningful relationships and the ability to make great contributions, whether of time, money, or both. Conversely, some of the unhappiest people are those who have the ability to buy anything, do anything, and go anywhere, but who have no one to enjoy anything with...and no meaningful purpose in their activities.

True abundance is not meant to benefit only oneself, but to touch a multitude of people. When Jesus and the disciples were seeking food while ministering to the masses, Jesus made a point not just to feed himself and his disciples, but to feed the masses as well. Abundance is overflow, and overflow has the expression of spilling over and pouring out goodness that can touch others.

Abundance Is a Choice

"Give, and it will be given to you, a good measure pressed down, shaken together, and running over, will be poured into your lap. For the measure you use will be the measure you receive." Luke 6:38

You invite abundance into your life by choosing to give of your life. At its root, abundance is about sacrifice. It models Christ-like humility. Christ humbled himself and gave his life away; He was given the greatest position in Heaven.

Far too often, we assume giving needs to be monetary, but the greatest gifts to others often cannot be measured---gifts like love, joy, peace, gentleness, grace and mercy. Truly what a man sows, he will also reap. If I am sowing seeds of love, I will invite and receive love. If I sow seeds of hate, I will receive hate. So the million dollar question is: What are you giving away to others? If abundance, then you will receive abundance. If lack and a spirit of stinginess, then you will receive lack. Our outward lives mirror who we are within. So, if you want abundance then put on a spirit of abundance.

What does a spirit of abundance look like?

A spirit of abundance gives freely, loves freely, and shares freely. It is not jealous, envious, and territorial, it neither hoards nor withholds. Philippians 2:4-8 best depicts a spirit of abundance:

   Transformed Through *His* Thoughts

Each of you should be concerned not only about your own interests, but about the interests of others as well. You should have the same attitude toward one another that Christ Jesus had who, though he existed in the form of God, did not regard equality with God as something to be grasped, but emptied (poured out) himself by taking on the form of a slave, by looking like other men, and by sharing in human nature. He humbled himself, by becoming obedient to the point of death—even death on a cross!

A spirit of abundance has the mind set to give away, to pour out and to empty yourself, because you know that God will fill you up!

"You prepare a table before me in the presence of my enemies. you anoint my head with oil; my cup overflows." Psalm 23:5

A spirit of abundance begins with an inward heart of humility, love, and giving. In Matthew 7:15-20, Jesus said, "Watch out for fake prophets who come to you in sheep's clothing but inwardly are voracious wolves. You will recognize them by their fruit. Grapes are not gathered from thorns or figs from thistle, are they? In the same way, every good tree bears good fruit, but the bad tree bears bad fruit. Nor does a bad tree bear good fruit. Every tree that does not bear good fruit is cut down and thrown into the fire. So then, you will recognize them by their fruit."

The true test of the person I am is the fruit I produce.

What kind of fruit do you produce? Is it the fruit of poverty by giving away hatred, slander, malice, disunity, and death? Look around you...look into the face of those closest to you---your wife, children, family, and co-workers to see the reflection of what type of spirit you are projecting and inviting back into yourself.

The opposite of poverty is abundance. Abundance is a

state of plenty, more than enough and overflowing. Satan is the god of lack—he comes to kill, steal, and destroy. (John 10:10) He wants to take from, not give to. He wants to take from us spiritually, emotionally, relationally, and financially. On the other hand, God wants to give to us. He wants to give us, above all else, eternal life, but also spiritual, emotional, relational, and financial wealth. Satan wants you to experience leanness, while God wants you to experience lavishness. Note: I am not saying that we will always experience abundance, because God can and does use seasons of leanness to produce lavish spiritual, emotional, relational, and financial blessings. But the key is never to forget that the primary source of abundance comes from God. "All wealth and honor come from the Lord." (1 Chronicles 29) The foundation to having abundance is to seek God. Matt 6:33 says, "Seek ye first the kingdom of God and all these things shall be added to you."

The second component to abundance is trust. God's principles are true, and the truth will set you free...but you will never apply His truths if you do not trust them. Since God's truths go against our natural grain, sometimes it is not easy for us. In fact, it is extremely hard. It would be as counterintuitive as saying "if you want to get straight A's don't study." You say, "Now what sense does that make?" But Isaiah 55:8 says, "My thoughts are not your thoughts neither are my ways your ways."

This principle is demonstrated when God tells us to give, and by giving He will give us a double portion. From a natural perspective, it would only be logical to conclude that the more I give, the less I have. Yet God is proposing that when you give to Him and his cause, he multiplies you. Perhaps we can say he releases abundance upon you. A good example is the story of Elijah, who told the destitute widow to use the last of her oil to make him some bread. She had only enough for herself and her son to make one more cake, but when she obeyed God's word, He gave her enough oil for life.

Abundance and poverty are both states of mind as much

                                    Transformed Through *His* Thoughts

as they are fiscal states. As your mind goes, so goes your life. Remember the wisdom of Solomon? "As a man thinks, so is he." The sad reality is that a majority of believers have a state of mind that says money is evil and that an over abundance of money will corrupt. It is no surprise that they are broke. There is nothing Godly about being poor. Sure it may be easier to be humble and dependant upon God in a state of lack, but you could easily say it is easier to be grateful and thankful in a state of abundance.

There is nothing godly about being poor from a financial perspective. However, to be poor in spirit is the primary duty of every believer. For Jesus said, *"Blessed are the poor in spirit, for the Kingdom of heaven belongs to them."* Jesus clearly communicates that those who humble themselves will experience his grace. Peter preaches this same concept in I Peter 5:5b when he says, *"God opposes the proud but gives grace to the humble."*

To avoid any confusion do not believe that your ability to obtain wealth will solve all your problems. There could be nothing further from the truth. But your ability to depend fully and solely upon God with a spirit of humility is the surest way to experience Gods grace and provision.

Larry Burkett was the founder and president of Christian Financial Concepts. In his book, How to Manage Your Money he defines wealth:

"Wealth is neither moral nor immoral. There is no inherent virtue in poverty there are dishonest poor as well as rich. God condemns the misuse of or preoccupation with wealth–not the wealth itself. The production of wealth is implied in Romans 12:5,8 where the gift of giving is listed as a Spiritual gift." (Burkett, p. 13.)

Solomon in Ecclesiastes 10:19, makes reference to the ruler who lives an undisciplined life and has the belief that money is the solution to their every problem. That wealth can simply bail them out, when they say, "money answers everything."

Yes, money is the primary form of exchange for services. Yet, only God himself is the answer to everything. Money can do nothing to heal the broken-hearted, money cannot solve the loss of a loved one, money cannot impart integrity, loyalty or chastity.

Paul said it best in Philippians 4:10-14, when he wisely stated, *"I have great joy in the Lord because now at last you have again expressed your concern for me. I am not saying this because I am in need, for I have learned to be content in any circumstance. I have experienced times of need and times of abundance. In any and every circumstances I have learned the secret of contentment, whether I go satisfied or hungry, have plenty or nothing. I am able to do all things through the one who strengthens me."*

The key to being victorious over poverty is learning to be content whatever your financial state. There must be at your core an inward trust, confidence and faith that God will provide for his children.

The Bible displays illustrations of how God provided for those with lack and those who experienced abundance.

Exodus 16:35 reveals a very liberating concept that displays God as Jehovah Jireh ("God Provides"). It states that the children of Israel ate manna for forty years as they wandered in the wilderness. Here is a clear illustration that, if you find yourself in a state of great lack, that God knows, sees, and is able to provide. No it wasn't T-bone steaks and the finest delicacies, but it met their needs.

R.B. Thieme, Jr. vividly depicts the children of Israel's journey in The Faith-Rest Life.

"The children of Israel had many pressures, problems, and needs. All during that time God had graciously and faithfully provided every logistical need that the Jews had for their wilderness journey. If they needed shoes, and they did, He supplied them. If they needed water, and they did, He supplied it. If they needed knowledge of military science to defeat their enemies, He supplied it. If they needed food, and they did, He

Transformed Through *His* Thoughts

supplied it. He also supplied the doctrine necessary to grow spiritually. He met every need that they had for forty years. For forty years the children of Israel had seen nothing but the faithfulness and grace of God!" (Thieme, p. 9.)

Don't allow Satan to keep you in a constant state of frustration if your finances are lacking. Remind yourself that God is faithful and gracious and if He can provide for the children of Israel surely He can provide for you.

However, if you find yourself in a state of abundance, don't be fooled---you have experienced this wealth not due to your own doing but because God has poured out his blessings upon you.

Consider Isaac in Genesis 26:12-14, *"When Isaac planted in that land, he reaped in the same year a hundred times what he had sown **because the Lord blessed him**. The man became wealthy. His influence continued to grow until he became very prominent. He had so many sheep and cattle and such a great household of servants that the Philistines became jealous of him."*

Perhaps we have confused abundance with greed and lack with godliness. The equation "abundance=greed" is not a valid calculation, neither is the equation "lack=godliness." For you can have greed without actually having abundance and you can have lack without righteousness. Greed is a characteristic that the Bible highlights as evil and destructive.

"Keep your lives free from the love of money and be content with what you have, because God has said, 'Never will I leave you; never will I forsake you.'"
Hebrews 13:5

We see here that the issue of greed is actually rooted in fear, the fear of not having enough. This attitude creates a spirit of hoarding and becoming overly possessive. But God wants His children to be free of fear and to give freely to others, so He reminds us that He provides all of our needs promises that He always will. But if we choose to love money and fear lack,

God gives a strong warning. "For the love of money is a root of all kinds of evil. Some people, eager for money, have wandered from the faith and pierced themselves with many griefs." (1 Tim 6:10)

The concept is not that money is evil, but greediness—when money becomes your sole and primary objective, exclusive from seeking first the kingdom of God—It is evil.

We must break the spirit of hoarding. It has been my observation that the greediest of people are those who have nothing. Those who have little tend to covet, hoard, and control. Their mentality is one of lack, so they go to all-you-can-eat buffets and eat like they will never eat again. Have you ever observed those receiving free gifts or food? Often they gather up as much as they can like a flock of wild birds---hoarding everything they can get their hands on.

Abundance has the mentality to give freely, the concept that there is plenty so I do not have to get it all today. People who have a spirit of abundance live in a state of trust and freedom, while the impoverished thinker lives in fear that tomorrow will be filled with lack.

We find a similar situation in the children of Israel, when God had them in the wilderness. He promised that He would supply their needs, daily. However, because they had a slave-and-lack mentality, they tried to hoard, covet, and control. When they acted out of that "lack mentality," by gathering extra manna–even though God had warned them against this so they could save it for another day, God spoiled the abundance. The abundance mentality focuses only on what you need now. God will supply your "now needs," so relax, trust and enjoy your situation today.

This is not to say we should not save, invest, and plant so we can reap and harvest. It is saying do not lose sight of the main thing: to seek first His kingdom and then all the other necessary things will be added. The beautiful truth is that God is an abundant God. He wants us to prosper in all aspects.

Although God wants us to prosper in all aspects, there is only one true way to be prosperous and that is through a personal relationship with Jesus Christ. Solomon in the book of Ecclesiastes closes with a solemn insight, *"Vanity of vanities." says the preacher, "all is vanity!"* Ecclesiastes 12:8

Solomon becomes vulnerable and extremely transparent in the book of Ecclesiastes. He is like a elderly man warning us to not follow in his erroneous footsteps. He communicates that his lust for the things of the world stole from the riches of his soul and spiritual life. At the end of his life, he realizes that it was useless to excessively strive and chase after wisdom (1:12-18), pleasure (2:1-3), great accomplishments (2:4-17), and labor (2:18-23).

However, what he discovered in his journey was that instead of striving after more one should learn to be content in the Lord!

"There is nothing better for a man than to eat and drink and tell himself that his labor is good. This also I have seen, that it is from the hand of God. For who can eat and who can have enjoyment without Him?" Ecclesiastes 2:24-25

Jesus Christ warns against this vanity of pursuing the wealth the world offers in comparison to the true wealth, the wealth that God offers through His son, Jesus Christ in Matthew 16:24-27:

"Then Jesus said to his disciples, if anyone wants to become my follower, he must deny himself, take up his cross, and follow me. For whoever wants to save his life will lose it, but whoever loses his life for my sake will find it. For what does it benefit a person if he gains the whole world but forfeits his life? Or what can a person give in exchange for his life? For the Son of man will come with his angels in the glory of his Father, and then he will reward each person according to what he has done."

The believer's life is not a bed of roses, for there will be days of tribulation, there will be days of lack, days of abundance and days somewhere in the middle. However, as a follower of

Christ, our sight should never be on earthly treasure but treasures laid up in heaven. True abundance is not how much money one can accumulate on earth. True abundance is knowing Jesus Christ as your Lord and Savior. For what does it profit a person to gain the whole world and lose their soul?

What does your spiritual 401k look like?

In other words where will you spend eternity after you retire from this world? Salvation is free, because Jesus paid for our sins on the cross. God in His wonderful grace and infinite wisdom has made it free because he sacrificed his only son, Jesus Christ so that you and I could experience a spiritual relationship with God.

"For this is the way God loved the world: He gave his one and only son, so that everyone who believes in him will not perish but have eternal life." (John 3:16)

If you want to be delivered from spiritual poverty then:

1. Acknowledge that you are a sinner (Romans 3:23).
2. Acknowledge that God sent his Son to provide you access to Himself (Romans 5:17-19, John 3:16).
3. Accept the free gift of grace by faith (Ephesians 2:8-9; Romans 10:9-11).

Prayer of deliverance from spiritual poverty
to spiritual abundance:

Dear Lord,
I acknowledge that I am a sinner and that I fall short of your holy standards. I thank you for the sacrifice and provision of your son Jesus Christ who died, was buried and rose again on the third day. And by faith I ask you to forgive me of my sins and to be my Lord and Savior.
In Jesus name, Amen!

If you prayed this prayer, praise the Lord for you have made the most significant decision you could of ever made by accepting Jesus as your personal Savior. "For whom the son sets free, is free indeed." John 8:36

At the Heart of Transformed Through His Thoughts is the awesome truth that, at salvation, the believer is endowed with spiritual riches which will enable us to live a prosperous spiritual life if we constantly remind ourselves that "Christ lives within us!" (Galatians 2:20)

"Beloved, I wish above all things that thou may prosper and be in health, even as your soul prospers." (3 John 1:2)

Affirmation

Today I function in the spirit of abundance, overflow, plenty, more-than-enough and increase. Therefore, I will give freely, withhold nothing, and hoard nothing. I will refrain from grasping possessions, wealth, people, or things tightly for I have no needs beyond this very moment. Every need I have, or will ever have, has already been supplied by God. I want for nothing (Psalm 23); whatever I need, He will guide me to it or bring it to me. He is my provider, my supplier, and He has an endless reservoir of resources.

Today I will be a component of blessings. I can take nothing of this world with me, so I will spread my possessions of money, food, things, time, love, joy, kindness, goodness and meekness to all who are in need because my Supplier will never run out.

I am grateful, thankful and elated with what I have today. I am happy and rejoice with those who have their perfect family, perfect relationships, perfect home, perfect car, perfect employment, perfect body, and perfect blessings. Envy, covetousness, and jealousy are not welcomed in my spirit; they are banned from entrance into my being. For I rejoice with those who rejoice, and I rejoice with what my God has supplied me with this day!

Abridged Affirmation

Today I function in the spirit of abundance, overflow, plenty, more-than-enough, and increase. Therefore, I will give freely, withhold nothing, and hoard nothing. I will refrain from grasping possessions, wealth, people, or things tightly, for I have no needs beyond this very moment. Every need I will have has already been supplied by God.

Synergy Prayer

Dear Lord,
I thank you that you are the source of wealth and
honor. I thank you that you have promised to supply
all my needs according to the richness of your grace. I
thank you that you are Jehovah Jireh, my provider. I
thank you I don't have to fret or worry, but just as you
provide for the birds of the air and cloth the lilies of the
field, so will you provide for me. Now, by faith I accept
this truth because you said it; and because you said it, I
believe it, even if I can't conceive it. Amen

Closing Prayer...

It is my prayer that you now fully grasp just how powerful your thoughts are, for the wisest man who ever lived said, "As a man thinks, so is he." The most powerful thoughts you could ever have are thoughts that are God-breathed, which are supplied for our daily warfare like ammunition that often goes unused. The scriptures, when we set our minds on its truths, are our lifelines to spiritual and emotional healing.

What I have tried to communicate through this spiritual motivational resource is that a defeated thought leads to a defeated emotion, which leads to a defeated behavior. But a victorious thought leads to a victorious emotion, which produces victorious behavior.

I truly believe with every ounce of faith that if these truths and principles are applied they will transform your life!

Dear Lord,

I pray that the reader will be emotionally blessed and fully aware of the thoughts that prevent them from experiencing their full potential . I pray that the reader will put more trust in your Word than their feelings or what their eye's see. I pray that the reader will embrace their God given talent and express that talent in a worthy cause. I pray that the reader will come to know you as their Lord and Savior and that they will claim and walk in the vast promises you have blessed them with as a child of God.

With love and respect,

Guy

Feel free to make extra copys of this sheet to assist
in monitoring your daily transformation.

Daily Monitoring Sheet

Rate yourself at your current mental state based on a scale of 1 to 10, with 10 being excellent and 1 being poor. As you incorporate the concepts in Transformed through Thought, using the Spiritual Synergy Affirmation to align your thoughts with God's Word, continue to work on your mind until you are consistently rating yourself between 8 and 10. Please note there will be days that you seem to regress, but don't allow yourself, others, or Satan to discourage you. The road to change is bumpy, and it is almost never a straight path.

Date: Time:

Rating	Attribute
1 2 3 4 5 6 7 8 9 10	Healthy view of self vs. Low self-esteem
1 2 3 4 5 6 7 8 9 10	Forgiving spirit vs. Unforgiving spirit
1 2 3 4 5 6 7 8 9 10	Love toward others vs. Anger toward others
1 2 3 4 5 6 7 8 9 10	Joy vs. Depression/sadness
1 2 3 4 5 6 7 8 9 10	Courageous spirit vs. Fearful personality
1 2 3 4 5 6 7 8 9 10	Patience vs. Impatience
1 2 3 4 5 6 7 8 9 10	Abundance vs. Lack and poverty
1 2 3 4 5 6 7 8 9 10	
1 2 3 4 5 6 7 8 9 10	
1 2 3 4 5 6 7 8 9 10	
1 2 3 4 5 6 7 8 9 10	
1 2 3 4 5 6 7 8 9 10	
1 2 3 4 5 6 7 8 9 10	
1 2 3 4 5 6 7 8 9 10	Overall Performance of logging my progress

Please make notes to express how you feel you can improve. Also in the blanks you can list other attributes you desire to improve on and create your own affirmations.

Daily Monitoring Sheet

Date: Time:

Scale	Item
1 2 3 4 5 6 7 8 9 10	Healthy view of self vs. Low self-esteem
1 2 3 4 5 6 7 8 9 10	Forgiving spirit vs. Unforgiving spirit
1 2 3 4 5 6 7 8 9 10	Love toward others vs. Anger toward others
1 2 3 4 5 6 7 8 9 10	Joy vs. Depression/sadness
1 2 3 4 5 6 7 8 9 10	Courageous spirit vs. Fearful personality
1 2 3 4 5 6 7 8 9 10	Patience vs. Impatience
1 2 3 4 5 6 7 8 9 10	Abundance vs. Lack and poverty
1 2 3 4 5 6 7 8 9 10	
1 2 3 4 5 6 7 8 9 10	
1 2 3 4 5 6 7 8 9 10	
1 2 3 4 5 6 7 8 9 10	
1 2 3 4 5 6 7 8 9 10	
1 2 3 4 5 6 7 8 9 10	
1 2 3 4 5 6 7 8 9 10	Overall Performance of logging my progress

Daily Monitoring Sheet

Date: Time:

Scale	Item
1 2 3 4 5 6 7 8 9 10	Healthy view of self vs. Low self-esteem
1 2 3 4 5 6 7 8 9 10	Forgiving spirit vs. Unforgiving spirit
1 2 3 4 5 6 7 8 9 10	Love toward others vs. Anger toward others
1 2 3 4 5 6 7 8 9 10	Joy vs. Depression/sadness
1 2 3 4 5 6 7 8 9 10	Courageous spirit vs. Fearful personality
1 2 3 4 5 6 7 8 9 10	Patience vs. Impatience
1 2 3 4 5 6 7 8 9 10	Abundance vs. Lack and poverty
1 2 3 4 5 6 7 8 9 10	
1 2 3 4 5 6 7 8 9 10	
1 2 3 4 5 6 7 8 9 10	
1 2 3 4 5 6 7 8 9 10	
1 2 3 4 5 6 7 8 9 10	
1 2 3 4 5 6 7 8 9 10	
1 2 3 4 5 6 7 8 9 10	Overall Performance of logging my progress

Daily Monitoring Sheet

Date: Time:

Scale	Item
1 2 3 4 5 6 7 8 9 10	Healthy view of self vs. Low self-esteem
1 2 3 4 5 6 7 8 9 10	Forgiving spirit vs. Unforgiving spirit
1 2 3 4 5 6 7 8 9 10	Love toward others vs. Anger toward others
1 2 3 4 5 6 7 8 9 10	Joy vs. Depression/sadness
1 2 3 4 5 6 7 8 9 10	Courageous spirit vs. Fearful personality
1 2 3 4 5 6 7 8 9 10	Patience vs. Impatience
1 2 3 4 5 6 7 8 9 10	Abundance vs. Lack and poverty
1 2 3 4 5 6 7 8 9 10	
1 2 3 4 5 6 7 8 9 10	
1 2 3 4 5 6 7 8 9 10	
1 2 3 4 5 6 7 8 9 10	
1 2 3 4 5 6 7 8 9 10	
1 2 3 4 5 6 7 8 9 10	
1 2 3 4 5 6 7 8 9 10	Overall Performance of logging my progress

Daily Monitoring Sheet

Date: Time:

Scale	Item
1 2 3 4 5 6 7 8 9 10	Healthy view of self vs. Low self-esteem
1 2 3 4 5 6 7 8 9 10	Forgiving spirit vs. Unforgiving spirit
1 2 3 4 5 6 7 8 9 10	Love toward others vs. Anger toward others
1 2 3 4 5 6 7 8 9 10	Joy vs. Depression/sadness
1 2 3 4 5 6 7 8 9 10	Courageous spirit vs. Fearful personality
1 2 3 4 5 6 7 8 9 10	Patience vs. Impatience
1 2 3 4 5 6 7 8 9 10	Abundance vs. Lack and poverty
1 2 3 4 5 6 7 8 9 10	
1 2 3 4 5 6 7 8 9 10	
1 2 3 4 5 6 7 8 9 10	
1 2 3 4 5 6 7 8 9 10	
1 2 3 4 5 6 7 8 9 10	
1 2 3 4 5 6 7 8 9 10	
1 2 3 4 5 6 7 8 9 10	Overall Performance of logging my progress

Daily Monitoring Sheet

Date: Time:

1 2 3 4 5 6 7 8 9 10	Healthy view of self vs. Low self-esteem
1 2 3 4 5 6 7 8 9 10	Forgiving spirit vs. Unforgiving spirit
1 2 3 4 5 6 7 8 9 10	Love toward others vs. Anger toward others
1 2 3 4 5 6 7 8 9 10	Joy vs. Depression/sadness
1 2 3 4 5 6 7 8 9 10	Courageous spirit vs. Fearful personality
1 2 3 4 5 6 7 8 9 10	Patience vs. Impatience
1 2 3 4 5 6 7 8 9 10	Abundance vs. Lack and poverty
1 2 3 4 5 6 7 8 9 10	
1 2 3 4 5 6 7 8 9 10	
1 2 3 4 5 6 7 8 9 10	
1 2 3 4 5 6 7 8 9 10	
1 2 3 4 5 6 7 8 9 10	
1 2 3 4 5 6 7 8 9 10	
1 2 3 4 5 6 7 8 9 10	Overall Performance of logging my progress

Daily Monitoring Sheet

Date: Time:

1 2 3 4 5 6 7 8 9 10	Healthy view of self vs. Low self-esteem
1 2 3 4 5 6 7 8 9 10	Forgiving spirit vs. Unforgiving spirit
1 2 3 4 5 6 7 8 9 10	Love toward others vs. Anger toward others
1 2 3 4 5 6 7 8 9 10	Joy vs. Depression/sadness
1 2 3 4 5 6 7 8 9 10	Courageous spirit vs. Fearful personality
1 2 3 4 5 6 7 8 9 10	Patience vs. Impatience
1 2 3 4 5 6 7 8 9 10	Abundance vs. Lack and poverty
1 2 3 4 5 6 7 8 9 10	
1 2 3 4 5 6 7 8 9 10	
1 2 3 4 5 6 7 8 9 10	
1 2 3 4 5 6 7 8 9 10	
1 2 3 4 5 6 7 8 9 10	
1 2 3 4 5 6 7 8 9 10	
1 2 3 4 5 6 7 8 9 10	Overall Performance of logging my progress

Daily Monitoring Sheet

Date: Time:

1 2 3 4 5 6 7 8 9 10	Healthy view of self vs. Low self-esteem
1 2 3 4 5 6 7 8 9 10	Forgiving spirit vs. Unforgiving spirit
1 2 3 4 5 6 7 8 9 10	Love toward others vs. Anger toward others
1 2 3 4 5 6 7 8 9 10	Joy vs. Depression/sadness
1 2 3 4 5 6 7 8 9 10	Courageous spirit vs. Fearful personality
1 2 3 4 5 6 7 8 9 10	Patience vs. Impatience
1 2 3 4 5 6 7 8 9 10	Abundance vs. Lack and poverty
1 2 3 4 5 6 7 8 9 10	
1 2 3 4 5 6 7 8 9 10	
1 2 3 4 5 6 7 8 9 10	
1 2 3 4 5 6 7 8 9 10	
1 2 3 4 5 6 7 8 9 10	
1 2 3 4 5 6 7 8 9 10	
1 2 3 4 5 6 7 8 9 10	Overall Performance of logging my progress

Daily Monitoring Sheet

Date: Time:

1 2 3 4 5 6 7 8 9 10	Healthy view of self vs. Low self-esteem
1 2 3 4 5 6 7 8 9 10	Forgiving spirit vs. Unforgiving spirit
1 2 3 4 5 6 7 8 9 10	Love toward others vs. Anger toward others
1 2 3 4 5 6 7 8 9 10	Joy vs. Depression/sadness
1 2 3 4 5 6 7 8 9 10	Courageous spirit vs. Fearful personality
1 2 3 4 5 6 7 8 9 10	Patience vs. Impatience
1 2 3 4 5 6 7 8 9 10	Abundance vs. Lack and poverty
1 2 3 4 5 6 7 8 9 10	
1 2 3 4 5 6 7 8 9 10	
1 2 3 4 5 6 7 8 9 10	
1 2 3 4 5 6 7 8 9 10	
1 2 3 4 5 6 7 8 9 10	
1 2 3 4 5 6 7 8 9 10	
1 2 3 4 5 6 7 8 9 10	Overall Performance of logging my progress

Daily Monitoring Sheet

Date: Time:

1 2 3 4 5 6 7 8 9 10	Healthy view of self vs. Low self-esteem
1 2 3 4 5 6 7 8 9 10	Forgiving spirit vs. Unforgiving spirit
1 2 3 4 5 6 7 8 9 10	Love toward others vs. Anger toward others
1 2 3 4 5 6 7 8 9 10	Joy vs. Depression/sadness
1 2 3 4 5 6 7 8 9 10	Courageous spirit vs. Fearful personality
1 2 3 4 5 6 7 8 9 10	Patience vs. Impatience
1 2 3 4 5 6 7 8 9 10	Abundance vs. Lack and poverty
1 2 3 4 5 6 7 8 9 10	
1 2 3 4 5 6 7 8 9 10	
1 2 3 4 5 6 7 8 9 10	
1 2 3 4 5 6 7 8 9 10	
1 2 3 4 5 6 7 8 9 10	
1 2 3 4 5 6 7 8 9 10	
1 2 3 4 5 6 7 8 9 10	Overall Performance of logging my progress

Daily Monitoring Sheet

Date: Time:

1 2 3 4 5 6 7 8 9 10	Healthy view of self vs. Low self-esteem
1 2 3 4 5 6 7 8 9 10	Forgiving spirit vs. Unforgiving spirit
1 2 3 4 5 6 7 8 9 10	Love toward others vs. Anger toward others
1 2 3 4 5 6 7 8 9 10	Joy vs. Depression/sadness
1 2 3 4 5 6 7 8 9 10	Courageous spirit vs. Fearful personality
1 2 3 4 5 6 7 8 9 10	Patience vs. Impatience
1 2 3 4 5 6 7 8 9 10	Abundance vs. Lack and poverty
1 2 3 4 5 6 7 8 9 10	
1 2 3 4 5 6 7 8 9 10	
1 2 3 4 5 6 7 8 9 10	
1 2 3 4 5 6 7 8 9 10	
1 2 3 4 5 6 7 8 9 10	
1 2 3 4 5 6 7 8 9 10	
1 2 3 4 5 6 7 8 9 10	Overall Performance of logging my progress

Daily Monitoring Sheet

Date: Time:

Scale	Item
1 2 3 4 5 6 7 8 9 10	Healthy view of self vs. Low self-esteem
1 2 3 4 5 6 7 8 9 10	Forgiving spirit vs. Unforgiving spirit
1 2 3 4 5 6 7 8 9 10	Love toward others vs. Anger toward others
1 2 3 4 5 6 7 8 9 10	Joy vs. Depression/sadness
1 2 3 4 5 6 7 8 9 10	Courageous spirit vs. Fearful personality
1 2 3 4 5 6 7 8 9 10	Patience vs. Impatience
1 2 3 4 5 6 7 8 9 10	Abundance vs. Lack and poverty
1 2 3 4 5 6 7 8 9 10	
1 2 3 4 5 6 7 8 9 10	
1 2 3 4 5 6 7 8 9 10	
1 2 3 4 5 6 7 8 9 10	
1 2 3 4 5 6 7 8 9 10	
1 2 3 4 5 6 7 8 9 10	
1 2 3 4 5 6 7 8 9 10	Overall Performance of logging my progress

Daily Monitoring Sheet

Date: Time:

Scale	Item
1 2 3 4 5 6 7 8 9 10	Healthy view of self vs. Low self-esteem
1 2 3 4 5 6 7 8 9 10	Forgiving spirit vs. Unforgiving spirit
1 2 3 4 5 6 7 8 9 10	Love toward others vs. Anger toward others
1 2 3 4 5 6 7 8 9 10	Joy vs. Depression/sadness
1 2 3 4 5 6 7 8 9 10	Courageous spirit vs. Fearful personality
1 2 3 4 5 6 7 8 9 10	Patience vs. Impatience
1 2 3 4 5 6 7 8 9 10	Abundance vs. Lack and poverty
1 2 3 4 5 6 7 8 9 10	
1 2 3 4 5 6 7 8 9 10	
1 2 3 4 5 6 7 8 9 10	
1 2 3 4 5 6 7 8 9 10	
1 2 3 4 5 6 7 8 9 10	
1 2 3 4 5 6 7 8 9 10	
1 2 3 4 5 6 7 8 9 10	Overall Performance of logging my progress

Daily Monitoring Sheet

Date: Time:

1 2 3 4 5 6 7 8 9 10	Healthy view of self vs. Low self-esteem
1 2 3 4 5 6 7 8 9 10	Forgiving spirit vs. Unforgiving spirit
1 2 3 4 5 6 7 8 9 10	Love toward others vs. Anger toward others
1 2 3 4 5 6 7 8 9 10	Joy vs. Depression/sadness
1 2 3 4 5 6 7 8 9 10	Courageous spirit vs. Fearful personality
1 2 3 4 5 6 7 8 9 10	Patience vs. Impatience
1 2 3 4 5 6 7 8 9 10	Abundance vs. Lack and poverty
1 2 3 4 5 6 7 8 9 10	
1 2 3 4 5 6 7 8 9 10	
1 2 3 4 5 6 7 8 9 10	
1 2 3 4 5 6 7 8 9 10	
1 2 3 4 5 6 7 8 9 10	
1 2 3 4 5 6 7 8 9 10	
1 2 3 4 5 6 7 8 9 10	Overall Performance of logging my progress

Daily Monitoring Sheet

Date: Time:

1 2 3 4 5 6 7 8 9 10	Healthy view of self vs. Low self-esteem
1 2 3 4 5 6 7 8 9 10	Forgiving spirit vs. Unforgiving spirit
1 2 3 4 5 6 7 8 9 10	Love toward others vs. Anger toward others
1 2 3 4 5 6 7 8 9 10	Joy vs. Depression/sadness
1 2 3 4 5 6 7 8 9 10	Courageous spirit vs. Fearful personality
1 2 3 4 5 6 7 8 9 10	Patience vs. Impatience
1 2 3 4 5 6 7 8 9 10	Abundance vs. Lack and poverty
1 2 3 4 5 6 7 8 9 10	
1 2 3 4 5 6 7 8 9 10	
1 2 3 4 5 6 7 8 9 10	
1 2 3 4 5 6 7 8 9 10	
1 2 3 4 5 6 7 8 9 10	
1 2 3 4 5 6 7 8 9 10	
1 2 3 4 5 6 7 8 9 10	Overall Performance of logging my progress

Daily Monitoring Sheet

<table>
<tr><td align="center">Date:</td><td align="center">Time:</td></tr>
<tr><td>1 2 3 4 5 6 7 8 9 10</td><td>Healthy view of self vs. Low self-esteem</td></tr>
<tr><td>1 2 3 4 5 6 7 8 9 10</td><td>Forgiving spirit vs. Unforgiving spirit</td></tr>
<tr><td>1 2 3 4 5 6 7 8 9 10</td><td>Love toward others vs. Anger toward others</td></tr>
<tr><td>1 2 3 4 5 6 7 8 9 10</td><td>Joy vs. Depression/sadness</td></tr>
<tr><td>1 2 3 4 5 6 7 8 9 10</td><td>Courageous spirit vs. Fearful personality</td></tr>
<tr><td>1 2 3 4 5 6 7 8 9 10</td><td>Patience vs. Impatience</td></tr>
<tr><td>1 2 3 4 5 6 7 8 9 10</td><td>Abundance vs. Lack and poverty</td></tr>
<tr><td>1 2 3 4 5 6 7 8 9 10</td><td></td></tr>
<tr><td>1 2 3 4 5 6 7 8 9 10</td><td></td></tr>
<tr><td>1 2 3 4 5 6 7 8 9 10</td><td></td></tr>
<tr><td>1 2 3 4 5 6 7 8 9 10</td><td></td></tr>
<tr><td>1 2 3 4 5 6 7 8 9 10</td><td></td></tr>
<tr><td>1 2 3 4 5 6 7 8 9 10</td><td></td></tr>
<tr><td>1 2 3 4 5 6 7 8 9 10</td><td>Overall Performance of logging my progress</td></tr>
</table>

Daily Monitoring Sheet

<table>
<tr><td align="center">Date:</td><td align="center">Time:</td></tr>
<tr><td>1 2 3 4 5 6 7 8 9 10</td><td>Healthy view of self vs. Low self-esteem</td></tr>
<tr><td>1 2 3 4 5 6 7 8 9 10</td><td>Forgiving spirit vs. Unforgiving spirit</td></tr>
<tr><td>1 2 3 4 5 6 7 8 9 10</td><td>Love toward others vs. Anger toward others</td></tr>
<tr><td>1 2 3 4 5 6 7 8 9 10</td><td>Joy vs. Depression/sadness</td></tr>
<tr><td>1 2 3 4 5 6 7 8 9 10</td><td>Courageous spirit vs. Fearful personality</td></tr>
<tr><td>1 2 3 4 5 6 7 8 9 10</td><td>Patience vs. Impatience</td></tr>
<tr><td>1 2 3 4 5 6 7 8 9 10</td><td>Abundance vs. Lack and poverty</td></tr>
<tr><td>1 2 3 4 5 6 7 8 9 10</td><td></td></tr>
<tr><td>1 2 3 4 5 6 7 8 9 10</td><td></td></tr>
<tr><td>1 2 3 4 5 6 7 8 9 10</td><td></td></tr>
<tr><td>1 2 3 4 5 6 7 8 9 10</td><td></td></tr>
<tr><td>1 2 3 4 5 6 7 8 9 10</td><td></td></tr>
<tr><td>1 2 3 4 5 6 7 8 9 10</td><td></td></tr>
<tr><td>1 2 3 4 5 6 7 8 9 10</td><td>Overall Performance of logging my progress</td></tr>
</table>

Daily Monitoring Sheet

Date: Time:

Scale	Item
1 2 3 4 5 6 7 8 9 10	Healthy view of self vs. Low self-esteem
1 2 3 4 5 6 7 8 9 10	Forgiving spirit vs. Unforgiving spirit
1 2 3 4 5 6 7 8 9 10	Love toward others vs. Anger toward others
1 2 3 4 5 6 7 8 9 10	Joy vs. Depression/sadness
1 2 3 4 5 6 7 8 9 10	Courageous spirit vs. Fearful personality
1 2 3 4 5 6 7 8 9 10	Patience vs. Impatience
1 2 3 4 5 6 7 8 9 10	Abundance vs. Lack and poverty
1 2 3 4 5 6 7 8 9 10	
1 2 3 4 5 6 7 8 9 10	
1 2 3 4 5 6 7 8 9 10	
1 2 3 4 5 6 7 8 9 10	
1 2 3 4 5 6 7 8 9 10	
1 2 3 4 5 6 7 8 9 10	
1 2 3 4 5 6 7 8 9 10	Overall Performance of logging my progress

Daily Monitoring Sheet

Date: Time:

Scale	Item
1 2 3 4 5 6 7 8 9 10	Healthy view of self vs. Low self-esteem
1 2 3 4 5 6 7 8 9 10	Forgiving spirit vs. Unforgiving spirit
1 2 3 4 5 6 7 8 9 10	Love toward others vs. Anger toward others
1 2 3 4 5 6 7 8 9 10	Joy vs. Depression/sadness
1 2 3 4 5 6 7 8 9 10	Courageous spirit vs. Fearful personality
1 2 3 4 5 6 7 8 9 10	Patience vs. Impatience
1 2 3 4 5 6 7 8 9 10	Abundance vs. Lack and poverty
1 2 3 4 5 6 7 8 9 10	
1 2 3 4 5 6 7 8 9 10	
1 2 3 4 5 6 7 8 9 10	
1 2 3 4 5 6 7 8 9 10	
1 2 3 4 5 6 7 8 9 10	
1 2 3 4 5 6 7 8 9 10	
1 2 3 4 5 6 7 8 9 10	Overall Performance of logging my progress

References

Allen, James (1998). As You Think. Novato, California: New World Library.

Amen, Daniel, G. (1998). Change Your Brain Change Your Life. New York: Three Rivers Press.

Burkett, Larry (1991). How To Manage Your Money. Chicago: Moody Press.

Chadwick, H., & Freeman J. (1998). Manners And Customs Of The Bible. Gainesville, Florida.

Covey, Steven, R. (1989). The Seven Habits of Highly Effective People. New York: Simon & Schuster.

Erickson, Millard (1985). Christian Theology. Grand Rapids: Baker Book House.

Frankl, Victor, E. (2006). Man's Search for Meaning. Boston: Beacon Press.

Hill, Napolean (1960). Think and Grow Rich. New York: Napolean Hill Foundation.

Helmstetter, Shad (1982). What to Say When You Talk to Yourself. New York: Simon and Schuster.

Thieme, R.B. Jr. (2004). The Faith-Rest Life. Houston, Texas: R.B. Thieme, JR., Bible Ministries.

Tolle, Eckhart (1999). The Power of Now. Novato, California: Namaste Publishing and New World Library.

Wood, S., Wood, E.G, & Boyd, D. (2004). Mastering the World of Psychology. New York: Pearson Education, Inc.

Zane, Frank http://frankzane.com/spring_1999.htm The Offical Frank Zane Website.

Photo by Kimberlee Rhames

Guy E. Earle began his counseling career as the staff counselor for the Urban Alternative radio program in 1995. Presently he serves as the Director of Counseling for Oak Cliff Bible Fellowship in Dallas, Texas - an 8,000 member congregation - where Dr. Tony Evans is the senior pastor. Guy earned a Master's degree in Theology and Pastoral Counseling from Dallas Theological Seminary, a Master's in Marriage and Family Counseling from Southwestern Baptist Theological Seminary. As an inspirational speaker and licensed professional counselor, he finds his greatest joy in seeing lives transformed to the likeness of Christ.

For more information or to contact Guy, please visit www.thegeegroup.com.

38953063R00079

Made in the USA
Lexington, KY
18 May 2019